LESSONS *from* LUCY

The Simple Joys of an Old, Happy Dog

DAVE BARRY

Simon & Schuster

New York   London   Toronto   Sydney   New Delhi

Simon & Schuster
1230 Avenue of the Americas
New York, NY 10020

First Simon & Schuster hardcover edition April 2019

SIMON & SCHUSTER and colophon are registered trademarks of Simon & Schuster, Inc.

For information about special discounts for bulk purchases, please contact Simon & Schuster Special Sales at 1-866-506-1949 or business@simonandschuster.com.

The Simon & Schuster Speakers Bureau can bring authors to your live event. For more information or to book an event, contact the Simon & Schuster Speakers Bureau at 1-866-248-3049 or visit our website at www.simonspeakers.com.

Interior design by Carly Loman

Manufactured in the United States of America

10 9 8 7 6 5 4

Library of Congress Cataloging-in-Publication Data

Names: Barry, Dave.
Title: Lessons from Lucy : the simple joys of an old, happy dog / Dave Barry.
Description: First Simon & Schuster hardcover edition. | New York :
    Simon & Schuster, October 2018.
Identifiers: LCCN 2018003591 (print) | LCCN 2018010287 (ebook) |
    ISBN 9781501161179 (Ebook) | ISBN 9781501161155 (hardback)
Subjects: LCSH: Conduct of life--Humor. | Aging--Humor. | Pets--Humor. |
    American wit and humor. | BISAC: HUMOR / Topic / Animals. | PETS /
    Dogs / General.
Classification: LCC PN6231.C6142 (ebook) | LCC PN6231.C6142 B38 2018
    (print) | DDC 818/.602--dc23
LC record available at https://lccn.loc.gov/2018003591

ISBN 978-1-5011-6115-5
ISBN 978-1-5011-6117-9 (ebook)

CONTENTS

LESSONS
from LUCY

INTRODUCTION

I've always been a dog person. When I was a boy our family had a standard poodle named Mistral, which is a French word for a cold northwesterly wind. The name wasn't our idea. Nobody in my family had ever been to France; we were the kind of family who would name a dog Buster. Mistral was named by his previous owners, a wealthy family who gave him to us because they could no longer keep him. When we got him, he was a pampered indoor dog who had one of those professional poodle hairstyles with the ridiculous poofs, including one on his head. I believe Mistral was embarrassed about how he looked, as if he'd gotten invited to a dog party where the invitation said, "Come in a wacky costume!" and he was the only dog who did.

But after a short while in the Barry household, wrestling with us Barry kids and racing around in the woods and marshes behind our house and never receiving any kind of even semiprofessional grooming, Mistral was transformed from a foo-foo house dog into a red-blooded, slobbering, leg-humping, free-range American dog so shaggy and filthy that it would not have been surprising to see soybeans sprouting from his coat.

I had a special bond with Mistral because I illegally fed him under the table at suppertime. As a child I was a very picky eater; the only foods I really liked were vanilla ice cream and ketchup.[1] But we Barry children were not allowed to leave the table until we cleaned our plates. So I was in big trouble when my mother, an otherwise decent human being, decided to serve us brussels sprouts, which—this has been shown in laboratory studies—are actually the severed heads of Martian fetuses. I could not eat them. I could barely look at them. The rest of the family would finish supper and go watch *Gunsmoke* on the RCA Victor TV with the massive wooden cabinet housing an eleven-inch, black-and-white, no-definition screen, and I'd be stuck at the table, sitting in front of a plate of

---

1   Although usually not together.

cold green slimy alien spheres, an abused child with nothing to look forward to except a slow death by starvation.

That changed when we got Mistral. At suppertime he would camp underneath the table in front of me and wolf down anything I slipped him—meat, fish, pasta, the occasional napkin, even vegetables, including brussels sprouts. In those days there was a TV show called *Lassie*, wherein every week a boy named Timmy—who was, with all due respect, an idiot—would get stuck in a well, or fall into some quicksand, or get into some other dire predicament. Then his faithful collie, Lassie, would race back to the farmhouse and bark at Timmy's parents— who were not themselves rocket scientists[2]—until they finally figured out, with some difficulty ("What's wrong, girl? Are you hungry?"), what Lassie was trying to tell them, even though this happened *every single week*. So they'd go rescue Timmy, and everybody would praise Lassie for being a hero.

To my mind Mistral was way more heroic. Any dog can run around barking. But show me the episode where Lassie eats Timmy's brussels sprouts.

---

2 For example, Timmy was eventually replaced by an entirely new boy named Jeff, and they didn't even notice *that*.

So I was a dog lover from the start. Our next family dog after Mistral was Herbie, who was a mixed breed, a cross between a German shepherd and an aircraft carrier. He was *huge*. Fortunately he was also very affectionate, although sometimes his rambunctiousness intimidated visitors who didn't know that he was harmless.

"Herbie!" we would shout. "Put the UPS man down RIGHT NOW!"

And usually he would. *Good boy!*

In my adult years I've had a series of dogs, each of them, in his or her own way, the Best Dog Ever. For a while I even had two dogs: a large main dog named Earnest, and a smallish emergency backup dog named Zippy. I wrote a number of columns about these two, the gist of these columns being: "These are not the brightest dogs."

Take the matter of going outside in the morning. This is a very big thing for dogs, because it's a chance to race around sniffing to determine where other dogs have made weewee, so they can make weewee directly on top of those places. Every dog on Earth is engaged in a relentless never-ending struggle with every other dog on Earth to establish weewee dominance. It's an immense responsibility.

So anyway, I used to let Earnest and Zippy out via a

two-stage procedure. Stage One was, I opened the back door, which led to the patio. This patio was surrounded by a screen enclosure, which is necessary in South Florida to prevent the mosquitos from making off with your patio furniture. Earnest and Zippy would race across the patio to the screen door and wait there, eagerly, for Stage Two, which was when I opened the screen door, and they were able to sprint outside and commence weewee operations.

We used this procedure for several years; Earnest and Zippy totally understood it. Then, in 1992, Hurricane Andrew roared through our neighborhood, and when it was gone, so was the patio screen enclosure.

But the screen door was still there.

Just the door, standing alone in its frame at the edge of the patio, with nothing around it.

How do you think Earnest and Zippy responded to this new situation, when it was time to go out in the morning? If you're a dog person, you have already guessed. I'd open the back door, and the two of them would sprint to the screen door—which I remind you was surrounded by nothing—and *stand there, waiting for me to open it*. I swear I am not making this up. It took them a couple of weeks to fully comprehend that they no longer needed to follow the two-stage procedure for going outside.

Earnest and Zippy provided me with a lot of entertainment. They were a comedy team, like a low-IQ version of Abbott and Costello. Sometimes when I was working they'd settle down snoozing on opposite sides of my office door—Earnest usually inside with me, Zippy outside in the hallway. They'd lie quietly, sometimes for hours, while I tapped away on my keyboard.

Suddenly, one of them would be activated by something. Dogs do this; they'll be sound asleep, then, for no apparent reason, they'll leap up, barking furiously. My theory is that there's a Dog Satellite orbiting the Earth, emitting signals that only dogs can hear as it passes over. Whatever it was, one of my dogs, usually Earnest, would hear it and start barking. This would awaken Zippy, on the other side of the door. He assumed Earnest was barking at something important, so he would start barking and leaping against the door, trying to get it to open so he could come in and help Earnest bark at whatever it was. Hearing this, Earnest would assume Zippy was barking at something important, and she (Earnest was female) would start leaping against the door from her side, which would make Zippy even *more* excited.

Now the two of them were hurling their bodies against the door in an escalating frenzy of dog alertness, by which

I mean stupidity. They would keep this up until I got up and opened the door. Earnest would then bolt out of the office, barking; Zippy would charge into the office, also barking. The two of them would eventually conclude that there was no threat, or that they had scared it away. I'd close the door and they'd resume snoozing on opposite sides of it, and the office would be peaceful again, until the next transit of the Dog Satellite.

So Earnest and Zippy were not geniuses. But they were fine dogs, and I was sad when I lost custody of them via divorce. I then entered a period of doglessness that lasted for ten years. When I remarried, I tried repeatedly to convince Michelle that we needed a dog, but she had never had a dog and was firmly opposed to getting one. Her view was that dogs are dirty, smelly animals that bark and slobber and chew things and jump up on you and deposit turds all over your yard.

All of which is of course true.

"But dogs are affectionate," I'd argue. "They make great companions."

Michelle would respond that she preferred companions that did not display their affection by suddenly thrusting their snouts into your groin.

"But dogs are *funny*," I'd argue. To illustrate how

funny dogs are, I told her the story (this is a true story) about a boyhood friend of mine who had a dog named Boomer who, while riding in the car, saw another dog and jumped out the car window while the car was traveling at a fairly high rate of speed. Upon landing, Boomer broke a number of important bones. He had to wear casts during a long and difficult recovery. Finally he healed, and not long after, he was again riding in the moving car, and he saw another dog. With no hesitation whatsoever *he jumped out again.*

"Why is that funny?" said Michelle.

"Because he jumped out *again*," I said.

"Why did they have the windows down?" said Michelle.

"They never thought he'd jump out again," I said. "But he did! Ha ha!"

Somehow this line of argument failed to convince Michelle that we needed a dog. And so we were dogless, and I thought we would remain dogless.

Then we had Sophie. From the start Sophie *loved* animals, all animals, and they loved her. She gave off some kind of vibe that resonated with them. Butterflies—I am completely serious here—would land on her hand, or in her hair, and just *stay* there. Cats—*cats*—would seek her out and rub against her, purring. Once we were in a rain forest in Costa Rica, and we saw a baby deer, which looked like Bambi, only cuter, standing a little way off the trail. A crowd gathered to take pictures and go *aww*, and the baby deer, instead of running away, came out of the forest, went directly to Sophie and *licked her face*. I know this happened because I took pictures.

Naturally Sophie loved dogs. When she was a baby, she would toddle up to dogs, even large dogs, and throw her arms around them in a big happy hug. The dogs would wag their tails and lick her; if we'd have let them, they'd have carried her off and raised her in the canine faith.

So now I had an ally. Now Michelle was constantly hearing a nagging, whiny voice: *"Please* can we get a dog? Please please PLEASE??" There was pouting and sulking. Sometimes there was sobbing and screaming, and floor-pounding tantrums.

That was all from me. Sophie was much more mature about it, but it was obvious that she, too, really wanted a dog. Michelle tried to placate her with tropical fish, but a fish cannot match a dog's ability to sense and respond to your emotional state, as we can see from this chart:

Your Emotional State	Fish's Response	Dog's Response
You feel happy.	*Swim around.*	*Lick you.*
You feel sad.	*Swim around.*	*Lick you.*
You feel scared because armed robbers have broken into your home and tied you up.	*Swim around.*	*Lick the robbers.*

So Sophie and I kept working on Michelle, and finally, one evening at a sushi restaurant, possibly under the influence of green tea, she caved and said: "OK, we can get a dog." Sophie and I were so happy we almost broke our chopsticks.

We began the search that very night. We wanted a rescue dog, so we looked at rescue-agency websites, which had photographs of the available dogs with brief descriptions. There were some cute puppies; Michelle and I assumed that Sophie would want one of those. But the photo that caught her attention barely looked like a dog at all. It was a very low-quality image of a black dog. All that were really visible were the dog's eyes, which reflected the camera flash, so what you saw were these two glowing orbs surrounded by a black blob. It looked like the Demon Dog from Hell.

This dog, a female about six months old, had been found a couple of months earlier wandering loose in Miramar, Florida, with another dog. They had no collars, no tags, no identification; somebody had abandoned them to roam the streets. The rescue agency, Paws 4 You, called them Paris and Monaco, just to give them names. The one that caught Sophie's attention was Monaco. The description with her photo said "she couldn't be sweeter if she tried." It also said that she never ate food from the other dogs' bowls.

Michelle and I kept pointing out cute puppies, but Sophie kept going back to the hellish glowing orbs that were Monaco. We asked her if she was sure that was the one she wanted.

"It says she couldn't be sweeter if she tried," she said.

So we made an appointment to meet Monaco. We wanted to make sure Monaco would be good with kids, so we took along Sophie's friend Stella. When we got to the rescue agency a volunteer brought Monaco outside on a leash to meet us. She was still in the late stages of puppyhood, well on her way to being a good-sized, and very strong, dog. She was thrilled to have company. Tail wagging wildly, she towed the volunteer over to Sophie and Stella—she could have towed a freight train—and the three of them commenced a lovefest, rolling around the grass, Monaco licking the girls and lying on her back, paws in the air, while Sophie and Stella climbed all over her.

"I guess she's good with kids," I said to Michelle.

In theory we were going to wait until after this meeting to decide whether we wanted to adopt Monaco. In actual fact the decision was made the instant Sophie and Monaco laid eyes on each other. We now had a dog, whose new name, bestowed by Sophie, was Lucy.

When we brought Lucy home she quickly adapted, as dogs do, to her new environment, except for one element: photo albums. We have a lot of albums; Michelle usually makes one after we take a vacation. I don't know why they and Lucy could not coexist peacefully. Perhaps tens of thousands of years ago, Lucy's ancestors were attacked by primitive photo albums, which in those days were much larger and more aggressive than the ones we have today. Whatever happened, Lucy had not forgotten it, and on several occasions during her first few months with us we came home to find an album from one of our family trips chewed into small pieces, leaving little shredded fragments of our happy decapitated vacation faces smiling up from all over the floor.

When this happened we would discuss our concerns with her ("NO! NO!" etc.) and she would usually be good for a few days. But then one of our photo albums would do or say something to trigger her again, and another trove of precious vacation memories would be converted into small wads of chewed paper.

Eventually Lucy made peace with our albums and became a good dog. Except for the matter of the living room sofa.

This sofa, which was not inexpensive, is white, in contrast to Lucy, who is black. She also sheds a lot. She's like a low-lying cloud that is constantly drizzling little black hairs.

When the new sofa arrived, my wife, Michelle, explained to Lucy that she was not allowed on it. Michelle did this by pointing at the sofa and repeating "NO!" in a commanding voice thirty or forty times. "No" is one of the eight words that Lucy definitely understands, the other seven being:

Lucy
Walk
Ball
Chicken
Cookie
Sit
Bubbe

"Bubbe" refers to my mother-in-law, Celia Kaufman, who always gives Lucy a dog biscuit ("cookie") when she visits us. If you tell Lucy, "Bubbe's coming!" she will go to the front window to watch the street, awaiting Bubbe's arrival. She will wait patiently for as long as it takes—I believe she would stay there for days—because she knows that at the end of her vigil Bubbe will appear and give her a cookie. This makes Bubbe Lucy's favorite human, along with pretty much every other human on Earth.

Getting back to the white sofa: the first night we had

it, as we prepared to go to bed, Michelle reminded Lucy about the Official Policy by pointing to the sofa and saying "NO!" another thirty or forty times. Lucy listened attentively, looking at Michelle with a somber and alert facial expression. There is no question she was getting Michelle's message (specifically, "No").

Nevertheless, the next morning, we realized that somebody had been on the sofa, and all the evidence pointed to one suspect, whose name you have no doubt already guessed: Bubbe.

No, seriously, the evidence pointed to Lucy, as follows:

Exhibit A: There were seventeen million tiny black hairs on the sofa.

Exhibit B: These hairs were arranged into an arrow pointing directly at Lucy.

Exhibit C: Lucy, who clearly had just jumped off the sofa, was on the floor with her head down, not making eye contact, which is the technique she uses when she wants to render herself invisible to humans.

So Michelle discussed the situation with Lucy at some length ("NO!" "NO!" "NO!" etc.), then painstakingly cleaned all the hairs off the sofa. That evening she again explained the Official Policy to Lucy and, as an added precaution, used chairs and a coffee table to form a barrier in front of the sofa. But this failed to prevent Lucy—who, when she is motivated, has a vertical leap of twenty-seven feet—from spending the night on the sofa.

That was the beginning of the Great Sofa War, which was not a happy time. Every night Michelle, who is not a quitter, would lecture Lucy and barricade the sofa; every morning we would wake up to find a hairy sofa and Lucy flattened against the floor, a black rug of guilt. The household grew tense. I attempted to lighten the mood by suggesting that we could solve the problem by dyeing Lucy white, but Michelle was not amused.

Fortunately, before we had to resort to extreme measures—erecting a wall around the sofa and forcing the Mexican government to pay for it, for example, or hiring a guard dog to guard our sofa from our dog—we found a solution. Instead of barricading the sofa at night, we started putting small electronic devices on it. Lucy is deeply suspicious of anything that involves electricity. I don't know why. Maybe electricity smells bad. All I know is, if Lucy is trotting toward you, and you show her, say, a mobile phone, she will slam on the brakes and back away with an expression of alarm, as if you're holding a rattlesnake, or—this is even scarier, because it means bath time—a bottle of dog shampoo.

So now, at bedtime, Michelle arranges a variety of small electronic items—a guitar tuner, a remote control, etc.—on the sofa cushions. This has worked beautifully; each morning the sofa is as hairless as a frog's belly. I suspect that during the night Lucy conducts regular surveillance missions into the living room to determine whether the sofa situation has changed, only to be forced to retreat when she sees that the devices are still vigilantly manning their posts. I like to think that if Lucy gets too close, the guitar tuner emits a low but distinct electronic "No!"

So we have won the battle, but I'm not so naïve as to think the war is over. If, one night, Michelle forgets to position the devices, Lucy will be back on the sofa. Because she is also not a quitter, and I'm sure she hasn't changed her mind about where she should sleep.

But aside from that, Lucy has been—as most dogs are—the Best Dog Ever. Despite their differences on sleeping arrangements, she managed to convert Michelle from a person who thought dogs were unhygienic and yucky into a person who would willingly permit a dog—a dog that only minutes earlier could have been conducting a deep probe of its own butt, or chowing down on another dog's poop—to lick her passionately on the face.

Lucy also won over Michelle's mom, a.k.a. Bubbe, who is no pushover, by being an attentive audience for Bubbe's repertoire of traditional Spanish and Yiddish songs.[3] When Bubbe sings to her, Lucy sits utterly still, staring at Celia soulfully, as if deeply moved by the music. In fact she's probably thinking, *This is the person who gives me cookies! Maybe she will give me a cookie!* But whatever Lucy's thinking, Bubbe loves her.

So Lucy is family, the way dogs become family. She is around us all the time; she is the soul of our house. She follows us from room to room, waiting to see where we settle so she can settle nearby. When we say her name or reach down to pet her, her tail thumps the floor in a drumbeat of joy. When we leave the house, she follows us to the door and watches us go, sad but resigned. When we return home she's waiting right there at the door, and she greets us joyfully whether we've been gone for five minutes or five hours. She is always happy to see us, always happy to be touched, always wildly enthusiastic about going for a walk. *Always.* She

---

3 Michelle's family is Cuban-Jewish, or as they call themselves, "Jewbans." They didn't travel from Cuba to the US on rafts; they parted the Caribbean.

is—except when we leave, or it's bath time—a happy soul.

She's also getting to be an old soul. Lucy turns ten this year. Her once jet-black face is now mostly white, and she has developed droopy jowls, which give her a perpetual expression of Deep Concern:

We love Lucy's face, but not everybody sees what we do. Recently Michelle and I were taking Lucy for her morning walk when we encountered a woman walking a well-groomed, obviously purebred dog with strikingly pointed ears. The woman and I had the following exchange:

ME: What kind of dog is that?

WOMAN: A Belgian Malinois.

ME: It's a beautiful dog.

WOMAN: Thank you! *(She looks at Lucy.)* Have a good day!

But we don't care what anybody thinks. We think Lucy is beautiful, inside and out. Especially inside. I don't want to sound all Californian here, but there's something spiritual about dogs. If you've ever had a dog, you know what I mean; you can see it when you look into their eyes. Dogs aren't people, but they're not mollusks, either. Lucy is *somebody*. Lucy has feelings, moods, attitudes. She can be excited, sad, scared, lonely, interested, bored, angry, playful, willful.

But mostly she's happy. She sleeps more than she used to, and she moves a little slower, but her capacity for joy, her enthusiasm for life, does not seem to have diminished with age. Michelle and I often marvel at Lucy's ability to be happy, especially compared with our own. We know, when we stop to look at the big picture, that we should be happy, too: we're very fortunate people leading very good lives. But we hardly ever stop to look at the big picture. We're almost always looking at the little picture, which is a random collage of pesky chores, obligations and annoyances—deadlines, bills, doctor appointments, grocery lists, the insanely complex carpool schedule, the leak in the roof, the car with a tire that's losing air (not to be confused with the car that needs an oil change), the odor in the kitchen that we hope will go away on its own and not turn out to be a deceased rat in the wall like last time, and on and on. When we think about bigger things, they're usually things that worry us—disease, aging, death, politics, the economy, terrorism, the decline of the once-great American newspaper industry into a big frantic Twitter account.

So we spend a lot of time thinking about things that make us stressed and/or unhappy. Whereas Lucy never thinks about any of these things. Sometimes when I'm working I'll pause from tapping on my keyboard and look at her, sprawled on the floor at my feet, emitting extravagant dog snores and the occasional dog fart, not concerned in the least about her career, or the future, or who the president is, as long as he doesn't try to give her a bath.

I envy Lucy's ability to not worry about things. I once got a letter from the Internal Revenue Service stating that I was going to be audited and would be required to produce basically all my financial documents dating back to middle school. I totally freaked out. This letter was all I thought about for weeks. Whereas Lucy, if she got exactly the same letter, would react by sniffing it to determine whether it had been peed on by another dog, in which case she would also pee on it. That would be the extent of her concern. If the IRS sent armed agents to arrest her for noncompliance, she would be thrilled to have company. She would greet the agents joyfully at the door and sniff them and lick them and go get her squeaky toy so she could play the game where she runs around squeaking her toy as you try without success to take it from her. If the agents took her to prison, she would go happily. She would enjoy the car ride; she would enthusiastically greet and lick the prison guards; she would vigorously inhale the exciting new pee aromas of her fellow inmates.

She would not dwell on the fact that she was in prison. She would accept her new situation, whether it lasted a day or the rest of her life. She would find a way to make the best of it.

That's what Lucy does: she makes the best of things. She's way better at this than I am. I know much more than she does, but she knows something I don't: how to be happy.

And that's the idea behind *Lessons from Lucy*. This book represents my attempt to understand how Lucy manages to be so happy, and to figure out whether I can use any of her methods to make my own life happier. Because—not to get too dramatic—I don't have that much time left. I turned seventy, which means I'm the same age as Lucy is in dog years. She and I are definitely getting up there. If our lives were football games, we'd be at the two-minute warning in the fourth quarter. If our lives were movie credits, we'd be way down at the bottom, past the assistant gerbil wrangler. If our lives were Cheez-It bags, we'd be at the stage where you hold the bag up and tilt it into your mouth to get the last crumbs.

In other words: The End Is in Sight. Whatever time I have left, I want it to be as happy as possible. And I'm hoping Lucy, who is aging so joyfully, can teach me how. Obviously I'm not saying I should behave exactly like her. For example, it would probably be a mistake for me to lick an IRS agent. (Although for the record I definitely would, if it would help.)

But I really do want to learn what Lucy can teach me.

However much time I have left, I want to make the best of it.

I want to age joyfully, too.

THE FIRST LESSON FROM LUCY

People often ask what kind of dog Lucy is. For years we didn't know. We assumed there was some Labrador retriever in her, because Labs are super-friendly dogs that will mate with anything. There's probably Lab DNA in the British royal family.

Lucy does look vaguely Lab-ish, but not like a purebred Lab. She's a big, muscular, short-haired, long-tailed, floppy-eared dog. Before her face started turning white, she was jet-black except for white patches on her throat and feet.

After years of speculating, I finally decided to find out exactly what Lucy is, so I ordered a genetic testing kit from a company called Wisdom Panel. Their motto is "Dogs can't talk, but their DNA can." For the record, this is a lie: Lucy can talk. If we ever attempt to sleep past approximately 7:14 a.m., even on a weekend, Lucy barges into our bedroom, paws the bed and says, "Wake up! It's time to feed me and then take me outside to make an absurd number of separate weewees!" The way she pronounces this, it sounds like "Arrrooooowwwwwrrr!" But there is no question what she means.

Anyway, the DNA testing kit was basically two swabs, which, following instructions, I rubbed against the insides of Lucy's cheeks, then mailed back to Wisdom Panel, which conducts laboratory analyses of dog DNA. As you know, "DNA" stands for "Deoxyribobananafanafofafeefimoramalamadingdong acid," which is a kind of molecule that is found inside every single cell of every single living criminal, which is why they are always leaving samples of it behind at crime scenes. It is also found in all living plants and animals except Madonna, who had all hers surgically removed in an effort to maintain a more youthful appearance.

About a month later, I received the Wisdom Panel report on Lucy's DNA. It begins:

Congratulations!
Lucy is a Boxer, Dalmatian, Chow Chow, Golden Retriever Cross.

According to the DNA analysis, one of Lucy's parents was a boxer; the other was half dalmatian and one-quarter each chow chow and golden retriever. So Lucy is half boxer, a quarter dalmatian, one-eighth chow chow and one-eighth golden retriever. Or, to put it in technical dog-breeder terms, she's a BoxMatianChowTriever.

I decided that since I was having Lucy's DNA tested, I'd also do my own. I used a company called 23andMe, which gets its name from the fact that, as a standard human, you have twenty-three pairs of chromosomes, which are tiny invisible biology things that determine various characteristics of yours, such as your hair color, eye color, shoe color, zodiac sign, aisle or window preference, number of drinks before you are willing to participate in the Chicken Dance, etc.

The way you send your DNA to 23andMe is frankly disgusting: you drool into a test tube. Really. The tube has a line on the side, and you're supposed to drool into it until your saliva reaches that level. I was not aware that drool contains DNA, but apparently it does. Either that, or this is an elaborate ruse by the people at 23andMe, who actually obtain your DNA from your fingerprints on the test tube, and for some sick reason are collecting a vast supply of human saliva. Maybe they use it to fill a decorative fountain at the 23andMe headquarters. Or maybe they have some kind of bizarre ritual wherein they immerse their naked bodies in vats of drool. I don't know, and I frankly refuse to engage in unfounded speculation about the perverts running 23andMe.

What I do know is that several weeks after they received my drool, they sent me a report on my DNA. Its main finding—this came as quite a surprise—is that my biological father is Warren Buffett.

No, I'm kidding. Although since I mentioned Warren in this book, I think it would be a nice gesture on his part if he were to mention me in his will.

What my 23andMe report actually said is that my ancestors were 99.9 percent European—68.4 percent British and Irish, 8.5 percent French and German, 4.7 percent Scandinavian, 16.9 percent "Broadly Northwestern European" and 1.4 percent from elsewhere in Europe. The remaining tenth of a percent is West African and Oceanian. So I am basically a generic white guy. In the rich, spicy, infinitely varied and fantastically flavorful gumbo that is humanity, I am a teaspoon of vanilla.

I pretty much expected this, because both of my parents were WASPs from the Midwest. Still, I was hoping that the report would reveal that I had some more exotic strains in my DNA—Cherokee, Zulu, chow chow, Scientologist, *something*. But it was not to be. Probably the most interesting statement about me in the 23andMe report was the following, which I am not making up: "David, you are likely to be able to smell the asparagus metabolite in your pee."

The report puts the probability of my having this trait at 78 percent; as it happens I can, in fact, smell this particular odor. Apparently this is a genetic thing, and the folks at 23andMe seem to find it fascinating. They state: "Studies report that in some parts of the world, the majority of people can smell it, while elsewhere the majority of people cannot."

I don't know if I want to go on living in a world with places where the majority of people can't smell the asparagus metabolite in their pee.

Anyway, my ancestors almost all came from a relatively small area of the planet. Lucy's ancestors were more widespread: golden retrievers originated in Scotland; boxers in Germany; dalmatians in Dalmatia, which is in Croatia, which, as an American, I could not in a million years locate on a map, but it sounds exotic; and chow chows in China. I don't know if Lucy's genetic makeup has anything to do with the fact that she's so friendly and outgoing. But something caused her to turn out that way. Even though, as a puppy, she was abandoned to the streets, where she probably had some unpleasant experiences, she shows no fear of strangers, human or canine. She is determined to shower love upon everybody she gets anywhere near. And she is always making new friends.

Pretty much everybody loves Lucy. It's hard not to: she greets all visitors, whether or not she's ever met them before, by running up to them, tail wagging, and expressing her love for them with every inch of her quivering-with-happiness body. She is ecstatic when, for example, the bug man comes. Every South Florida household has a bug man who comes once a month to spray deadly carcinogens around as part of the ongoing battle between humans and what we call "Palmetto bugs," which are cockroaches the size of mature squirrels. Without the ceaseless efforts of the bug men, South Florida would be overrun in a matter of hours.

The bug man is Lucy's best friend. She follows him from room to room, ready and eager to assist in the event that he needs to be licked. She's like this with all visitors to our house; every one of them is her best friend. So is everybody she meets when we're out walking around looking for places to make weewee. She has many, many best friends. She loves everybody, and she assumes everybody will love her back. And she's almost always right.

Not all dogs are like this, of course. Some dogs don't seem to like anybody. These are usually your very small dogs, the kind that have to be transported in special dog-holding purses, because if they were ever to be set down on the ground they would be carried off by spiders. They need constant attention from their owners, and they can be very annoying. I refer here to the owners. The dogs are even worse, always yapping and growling, as if they're some kind of badass carnivore of the animal kingdom, instead of basically a paramecium with fur.

But larger dogs tend to be friendly, and Lucy is a larger dog. She emits poops the size of Yorkshire terriers. She is seventy-five pounds of pure, unstoppable affection, a powerful groin-seeking missile of love.

I am way, *way* less social than Lucy, despite having been raised in a supportive and loving family (except for the brussels sprouts). Maybe I inherited whatever gene causes the famous British reserve. Whatever the reason, my operating assumption, when confronted with people I don't know, is that I'm probably not going to like them. And the older I get, the more reluctant I am to meet new people, especially when I'm alone and don't have Michelle or somebody else I know to act as a go-between. When I'm alone in a social setting—say, a crowded hotel bar—I *never* strike up conversations. I'm the guy staring at his phone even though there's nothing to see on it, or pretending to be riveted by competitive lumberjacking on ESPN. In other words, I'm shy.

This is not my public image, of course. My public image is Mr. Wild and Crazy Humor Personality—always cracking jokes and kidding around, the kind of guy who does wacky things like picking up his son at middle school in the Oscar Mayer Wienermobile, or setting fire to a pair of underpants with a Barbie doll on national television. I have, in fact, done both of those wacky things, and many more like them. And when I do public events such as book signings and speeches, I am in fact Mr. Humor Personality—on the outside. But inside, believe me, I am shy. Like a lot of people who are funny for a living, I use humor for two reasons:

1. To get people to like me, because deep down inside I am still the geeky, deeply insecure glasses-wearing kid I was in fourth grade.
2. To wrap myself in a protective barrier of humor, sarcasm and wiseassery that will prevent people from actually getting to *know* me, because I fear that if

they *did* know me they wouldn't like me, because deep down inside I am still the geeky, deeply insecure glasses-wearing kid I was in fourth grade.

Over time, some people penetrated my humor barrier, and we became close friends. But this was mostly back during my college/rock band years, and my early years in the newspaper business, when everybody was having new experiences[4] together and every night was party night. I had a LOT of fun times, and the people I had them with became my close friends.

When I grew up and got married and became a dad, I became more focused on family. I spent less time having fun with my friends, and less time in settings where I might make new ones. I think this is the pattern for a lot of people, as they head into middle age. In my case it was intensified by the fact that, as I became successful in my writing career, many of the people I met expected me to be—even demanded that I be—Mr. Wild and Crazy Humor Personality. And I usually was, because it was easier than actually engaging with them, which meant they never really got anywhere near me, nor I them.

---

4   If you know what I mean.

The result is that, at age seventy, I *know* a ton of people, but I have few close friends, mostly people I met long ago. And the truth is, I hardly ever see or talk to them. For all I know, some of my close friends could be dead. The only way to find out would be to call them up and talk to them about what's going on in their lives, and I never do that.

I think this is true of many guys, even the ones who are not Humor Personalities: we do not view talking about our personal lives as an acceptable activity.

Imagine two people who are acquaintances, and who have both just been diagnosed with serious, possibly fatal diseases. Now imagine that they run into each other at a car wash, so that, while waiting for their cars, they spend a few minutes talking. If these people are women, they will immediately discover their common plight, and there will be tears and hugging, and possibly an immediate trip to Starbucks for commiserative chai lattes.

But if these two people are men, it's entirely possible that neither will mention his medical situation *at all*. It's entirely possible that their entire conversation will consist of dissecting a recent decision by an NFL quarterback— whom neither one of them knows personally or will ever meet—to throw a short pass to a running back on third and twelve when the deep receiver *was wide open for God's sake*. ON THIRD AND TWELVE!!!

Sometimes I think the main purpose of professional sports is to give guys something to talk about that does not involve them personally.

My point is that women tend to be better at making, and keeping, friends. My wife, Michelle, who is a woman, has dozens, maybe hundreds, of friends, and makes new ones regularly. Whenever she sees or hears from any of these friends, they have a conversation, usually involving their personal lives, that could easily last longer than dental school. She is closer to *all* her friends than I am to *any* of mine.

My seventeen-year-old daughter, Sophie, also has far more friends than I do, thanks largely to Snapchat,[5] which enables her to keep in constant contact with the entire seventeen-year-old population of the Western Hemisphere. And, like Michelle, she's constantly making new friends.

Whereas I am not. I am, through death and distance, losing and drifting apart from my friends. And what bothers me about this, when I stop to think about it, is that *it*

---

5   Whatever the hell that is.

doesn't really bother me. The older I get, the more accustomed I am to solitude. When Michelle and Sophie are off doing things, I can spend an entire weekend alone—making no effort to see or talk to anybody—and be perfectly content.

That's me: content. No complaints.

But . . .

I'm thinking I shouldn't settle for being content.

I think that, even at seventy, I should still be aiming to be happy.

Like my old—but still happy—dog, Lucy.

Which leads me to the first Lesson from Lucy, which is:

Make New Friends.
(And Keep the Ones You Have.)

Making friends, at this point, will not be easy for me, but I intend to try. When I meet new people, I'm going to make a conscious effort not to hide behind my humor barrier, nor use my age as an excuse to be a recluse. I'm going to think about Lucy—about the trustful, open, unreservedly joyful way she approaches everybody, and the happiness she clearly derives from her many friends. I'm going to think about that, and look these new people straight in the eye, and, with a positive, welcoming attitude, I am going to thrust my snout into their groins.

OK, no, I will not be emulating Lucy to that extent. But I am seriously going to try to be more open to new friendships. I am also going to make an effort—starting today—to stay in better touch with my old friends.

Between the end of that paragraph and the beginning of this one, I turned the computer on which I am writing this all the way off so that I couldn't distract myself with the Internet. Then I called Rob Stavis, whom I've known since the sixties, when we were students at Haverford College, where, on the night that he was accepted at the medical school of his choice, we celebrated by, among many other things, standing in the dormitory-bathroom shower fully clothed with the water running and drinking bourbon from a shoe that did not belong to either of us.[6] That's the kind of friends we were back then, and I still count him as one of my closest friends. But these days we don't talk much, and when we do it's almost always because he reached out to me.

So this time I reached out to him, and we talked for

---

6   If you must know, it belonged to John Cooper.

half an hour, which for me is a *very* long conversation. When we finally said goodbye, I felt really, *really* good, and I wondered why I didn't call him more often. I will make a point of doing that again, with him and with other friends. What the hell am I doing that's more important?

So that's my plan for being a friendlier, and I hope happier, me. I may even attempt to strike up conversations with strangers in bars. This could be tricky, because, as I said, I am fundamentally shy. I have little experience with conversation-starting small talk.

ME: Hi.

STRANGER IN BAR: Hi.

ME: I can smell the asparagus metabolite in my urine.

STRANGER IN BAR: Check please.

So OK, maybe I won't make my new friends in bars. But I *will* make some new friends.

THE SECOND LESSON FROM LUCY

Getting old sucks.

That's not the second Lesson from Lucy. Lucy is not aware that she's getting old. But for humans, it's a fact of life: getting old sucks.

Oh, sure, some people *claim* it doesn't suck. And by "some people," I mean AARP.

AARP, as you probably know, is the last sound you make before you die.

911 OPERATOR: This is 911. Do you have an emergency?

CALLER: Yes! It's my husband! He collapsed to the floor and his face turned blue and he's making a weird noise!

911 OPERATOR: What kind of noise?

CALLER: It sounds like "aarp."

911 OPERATOR: OK, I'll send a hearse.

CALLER: Don't you mean an ambulance?

911 OPERATOR: No.

"AARP" is also an abbreviation for "American Association of Retired Persons Standing in Line Ahead of You Demanding a Discount on Every Freaking Thing." AARP is a powerful lobbying group representing the interests of senior citizens. Like, if a member of Congress even *thinks* about cutting Social Security benefits, an elite AARP tactical assault lobbying squad will descend on the congressperson's office at a slow rate of speed and wave their catheters around in a threatening manner until the congressperson sees the light.

I have no problem with that aspect of AARP. I've been paying into the Social Security system since the French and Indian War, and *I want to cash in*. Yes, I am aware that Social Security is basically a giant Ponzi scheme, and that we baby boomers, as we retire in vast numbers and start collecting from the system, will be imposing an enormous, unfair and potentially ruinous financial burden on younger generations. I view this as payback for what the younger generations have done to music.

But I part company with AARP on the question of

whether or not aging sucks. AARP's official position is that it does not. The CEO of AARP, Jo Ann Jenkins, has a book, heavily promoted by AARP, titled *Disrupt Aging: A Bold New Path to Living Your Best Life at Every Age.* In this book, according to AARP, Jenkins "encourages us to re-think the negative stories we tell ourselves and each other about aging." AARP has a whole "Disrupt Aging" campaign going: the message is that society should abandon the stereotype that older people are crotchety clueless doddering old farts.

"Enough with dotty driver and goofy grandma memes!" states AARP. "The over-60 set is running corporations and ruling supreme courts, why is it still acceptable to group all elders as demented dimwits unable to use a TV remote?"

(AARP apparently believes that senior citizens are "ruling" supreme courts.)

"Age isn't a punchline," asserts AARP. "It's about growth. You aren't 'too old' for anything."

Oh really, AARP? I beg to differ. Those of us drifting into our seventies and beyond are definitely too old for some things. Public nudity is the obvious example. Some years ago my family and another family, both with young children, were on a Caribbean cruise that stopped for a day at

St. Martin. The island is divided into two sectors, a Dutch sector and a French sector. The Dutch sector is known for nightlife, by which I mean drinking. People on the Dutch side start engaging in nightlife as early as breakfast.

The French sector is known for nude beaches. That's the weird thing about the French. If you go to Paris, you'll find that everybody is dressed quite formally, at least by American standards. If you walk into a Paris restaurant attired in shorts and sneakers, the French will look at you as though you are wearing a Hefty trash bag. But when these same French people get to a beach, they immediately remove all their clothes and stroll around openly flaunting their legumes.

So anyway, we were on this St. Martin French beach with our small children, and no sooner did we settle onto our beach chairs than a herd of French people commenced parading past us stark naked. Some of these people were not unattractive to look at; these were your younger people. But the older naked people made you yearn for a total solar eclipse. There was a lot of drooping. The men, especially, were prone to extreme droopage in the groinular region, which as a human you do NOT want to see. There was one elderly man—I will never be able to completely erase this image from my brain—who was strolling toward us with his scrotal appendage dangling so low that a crab could easily have reached up a claw and grabbed it, although tragically this did not happen.

So no matter what AARP says, you can definitely be too old for public nudity. Also, if you're an older person who is not Mick Jagger, you are too old for "skinny jeans." Also older people should not unironically attempt to use millennial slang that millennials use to communicate to other millennials the information that they are millennial, such as "bae," "JK," "FOMO," "JOMO," "salty," "hepcat," "twenty-three skidoo," etc.

Commercial airline pilots are legally required to retire when they reach age sixty-five. At that point they're probably all still perfectly competent, but they have to stop anyway. Why do you suppose that is, AARP officials? If aging is about "growth," why not let these pilots keep right on growing and flying large planes into their seventies, their eighties, even their nineties?

> PILOT: Folks, we've reached a comfortable cruising altitude, so I'm going to go ahead and turn off the FASTEN SEAT BELT sign.
>
> *(All the engines shut down. The plane immediately starts losing altitude.)*

PILOT: OK, apparently we've begun our descent into Chicago.

Which leads us to the unfair stereotype that older people are confused by technology. Wherever did THAT crazy notion come from, AARP officials?

Let me suggest a possible answer, based on my experience as an author. When I have a new book out, I'll usually travel around the country making appearances in bookstores, where I'll give a short talk and then answer audience questions about my work, such as "Do you know Carl Hiaasen?" and "What is Stephen King really like?" After that I sign books for people who've bought them. Often people want to take pictures, which is of course very flattering; over the years I've posed for thousands of pictures, taken by people of all ages, almost always using cell phones. I have observed that young people and old people use very different picture-taking techniques.

YOUNG-PERSON TECHNIQUE

1. Hold up the phone.
2. Take the picture.

OLD-PERSON TECHNIQUE

1. Hold up the phone.
2. Frown at the screen for thirty seconds.
3. Say, "Wait, I think it's on Google."
4. Stab at the screen for a while with a forefinger.
5. Hold up the phone again and say, "OK! Smile!"
6. Frown and say, "Wait, I think it's making a video."
7. Stab at the screen some more.
8. Hold up the phone again and say, "OK! Smile!"
9. Frown and say, "Wait, it took a picture of me."
10. Hand the phone to a younger person, who takes the actual picture.

I have here several news reports from Webster Parish, Louisiana, concerning a sixty-one-year-old woman who is suing the Webster Parish Convention and Visitors Bureau to get her old job back. She was the parish's tourism director, but she was fired.

What happened, according to the reports, was that she was in Baton Rouge one evening on business, and she decided to livestream video of herself nude to her husband via Instagram. This was of course a totally OK, even admirable idea; speaking on behalf of all husbandkind, I say: God bless this woman. The problem was, she was using an iPhone 7 that she had been issued for work, and, as she told the *Minden Press-Herald*: "I am a new Instagram user and, unfortunately, I pressed the wrong button."

The result was that she broadcast thirty minutes of her unencumbered self on the official, and public, Instagram account of the Webster Parish Convention and Visitors Bureau. I like to think that this broadcast could actually have boosted convention and visitor business, that the concept developed by this woman could be used as part of a new tourism-promotion campaign ("Webster Parish: Check Out THESE Attractions!").

Instead the woman was fired. As I write this, she's suing on the grounds that the firing was done improperly. I hope she wins, because, as a senior citizen, I can easily imagine messing up an Instagram livestream video. Like millions of people my age, I don't really know what Instagram *is*. Every time I ask my daughter if she's on it, she looks up from her phone, rolls her eyes several linear feet and says, as if explaining something to an unusually stupid plant, "This is Snapchat." (Which is another thing I do not understand.)

I could present many more examples of seniors strug-
gling with technology, but I believe I've proved my point,
which is that AARP—an organization for which I have
the utmost respect—is full of shit. Aging is not "growth,"
unless you are referring to nasal hair. Aging is getting
old, and it sucks. Things that used to be easy—standing
up, for example, or remembering the names of your immediate family members—become increasingly difficult.

These are among the obvious reasons why getting old
sucks. One of the subtler reasons—and the subject (finally)
of this chapter—is that *you stop having fun.* You stop seeking fun experiences; you stop even remembering what fun
is. The fun has pretty much evaporated from your life, replaced by a focus on such matters as where your reading
glasses are.[7] But you tend not to notice the de-funning, because it happens so gradually. The truth is that the fun has
been slowly draining out of your life for most of your life.

I become acutely aware of this when I hang out with
my grandson, Dylan Maxwell Barry. He's three, and when
he's not sleeping or experiencing minor episodes of three-
year-old crankiness, he's having fun. It's what he does.
He's a small but potent nuclear reactor of fun.

---

7   Answer: on your forehead.

Dylan lives in a condominium building in New York City, at the end of a long hallway. To an old person such as myself, this hallway is just a random, nondescript passageway to be trudged through en route from the elevator to the condo and back. But to Dylan, the hallway is a wondrous space—a playground, a racetrack with lines on the floor that you can jump over, a tunnel with corners you can duck around and use for hiding. And at one end is an elevator that goes up and down and has buttons that you can push AND THEY LIGHT UP! Dylan uses that hallway maybe a half dozen times a day, and every single time he has more pure fun than I do in the average week. Dylan has fun *all the time.*

Pretty soon he'll start school. He'll still have fun there, especially early on, but he'll also start being exposed to non-fun activities as part of the educational process, and these activities will become less and less fun, leading, inexorably, to: the cosine.

Dylan's education will be followed by a career, and at some point probably marriage and family. These life stages will of course offer opportunities for fun, sometimes great fun, but this fun will have to be squeezed in amid the seemingly endless exhausting obligations of work and worry that overwhelm us grown-ups, wearing us down over the years, eroding our fun-having skills until we reach the point where it never would occur to us that a hallway has any purpose other than to get us from Point A to Point B.

For now, though, the hallway is still fun for Dylan. Almost everything is fun for Dylan. To him the world is still new, surprising, fascinating, full of wonders.

We old people have mostly lost that sense of wonder, which is why we respond viscerally—at least I do—when we hear Louis Armstrong sing "What a Wonderful World." It's a simple song with an obvious, even corny, message: the everyday world around us, the things and people we take for granted—flowers, friends, trees, babies—are pretty darned marvelous when we stop to think about them. But of course we don't stop to think about them, except when Louis Armstrong reminds us to. For the two minutes or so that the song is playing, we become mushballs, filled with wistful yearning and gratitude and sap. I think to myself: *Louis Armstrong is absolutely right—it IS a wonderful world.*

Then the song ends, and my mushy feelings linger for maybe another thirty seconds, and I remember that I have a bill to pay or an email to answer, and before long I am once again trudging obliviously down the Condominium Hallway of Life, heading for my inevitable rendezvous with the Elevator of Fate.[8]

I realize I'm not imparting original wisdom here. Every thinking adult knows what I'm talking about. Our existence on Earth is limited; we're reminded of this every time we attend a funeral. Yet as soon as we leave the cemetery we resume pissing away our remaining hours obsessing over what are mostly minor annoyances. We keep telling ourselves that someday we'll retire, and *then* we'll have time to enjoy ourselves. We'll have fun! But when we finally get to the point where we really could retire—I'm getting there now—we've forgotten how to have fun. We're out of practice.

You know who's not out of practice? Lucy. She's an old lady; she sleeps more than she used to, and she moves a little slower. But she is still *always* up for fun. If she sees another dog, she wants to play with that dog, once they have completed the formality of inhaling each other's butt fumes. If there's no other dog available, she wants to play with us humans.

She especially likes to play a game I call "ball,"

---

8   Which I hope will take me to the Penthouse of Paradise, and not the Sub-Basement of Eternal Damnation.

where the ball is any one of the many dog toys Lucy has acquired over the years. Some of these are actual balls, but they're also a wide range of other prized Lucy possessions—a rubber shoe that squeaks; mysterious sketchy-looking organic chew things that we buy at the pet store that for all we know could be human ligaments; a large, blue, bone-shaped stuffed toy she got for Chanukah[9] that says KOSHER; and a wide array of other stuffed chew toys, including dolls representing John McCain and Hillary Clinton. I was given these dolls as press freebies while writing columns about the 2008 presidential campaign; they were manufactured by a chew-toy company under the assumption that either McCain or Clinton would be the next president. (That's right: when it comes to predicting the outcomes of presidential elections, chew-toy companies are as incompetent as professional journalists.)

Lucy plays ball to celebrate all major household events. Let's say I open the drawer where we keep Lucy's leash. This is *huge*, because it means we're going outside, where we will have a chance to explore and savor the endlessly fascinating tapestry of weewee aromas. But we

---

9   Lucy is Jewish.

cannot go outside immediately, even though I am standing by the front door holding the leash, ready to go. First we must celebrate this exciting and exceedingly rare occasion that only happens three or four times per day by playing a game of . . . *ball*!

To initiate the game, Lucy sprints to the family room and roots urgently through her bucket of possessions—there are dozens in there—until she finds the one she's looking for. Say it's her John McCain doll. She grabs it in her teeth and races back to the front door. She skids to a stop a few feet from me and shakes her head violently, flaunting the doll, daring me to try to take it from her. My role in the game is to pretend that I find it highly desirable, even though if I am being perfectly honest it is, after years of use, a hideous drool-soaked wad of filth.

"Give me that!" I say, lunging at it. "GIVE ME JOHN McCAIN RIGHT NOW!!"

But Lucy does not give it to me. I have not earned it. She prances backward, brandishing John McCain in a taunting manner. At this point I am supposed to chase her. I don't *want* to chase her; I want her to let me put her leash on and take her outside to do her business so I can get back to my important adult human business of not having fun. I have tried training Lucy to drop the ball on command and come to me, but she is not big on commands. So I have no choice but to play ball. I lumber after her, shouting, "GIVE ME JOHN McCAIN!" as she prances gaily from room to room.

This can go on for several minutes. Eventually Lucy decides that she has won, thus extending her undefeated streak to 6,748 consecutive games of ball. She drops John McCain and permits me to put on her leash, and we go outside, where she has even *more* fun.

Going outside is not the only occasion for a game of ball. Lucy plays it whenever anything exciting happens. By "anything exciting," I mean "anything." Sunrise, for example. Or somebody entering the house, even if that person left the house fifteen seconds earlier. Or she happens to wander into a room and discovers John McCain lying on the floor from a previous game of ball. So what with one thing and another, Lucy—like Dylan—is always finding opportunities to have fun. This is yet another area in which Lucy is happier than I am.

So our second Lesson from Lucy is:

Don't Stop Having Fun.
(And If You Have Stopped, Start Having Fun Again.)

As was the case with the previous Lucy lesson—about making friends—I have not done particularly well in this area. You'd think I'd be having a lot of fun, seeing as how my job consists of being funny, or at least trying to be funny. But the truth is that being funny, when it's your job, is work. Ask any stand-up comedian.

I'm not saying professional humor is *grueling* work, like mining coal or cleaning toilets or being a personal assistant to a Kardashian. But generating humor for a living—although it can be interesting and challenging—isn't *fun*. You never, after working on a joke for forty-five minutes, find yourself thinking, *Ha ha! I am cracking my own self up with this humor!* Your thinking is more along the lines of: *Is it too late to apply to law school?*

Don't get me wrong: I've been very lucky in life, and I'm definitely content. But being content is not the same thing as having fun. I think contentment is what we older people too often settle for in place of fun. Note how older-person "fun" is depicted in the seventeen trillion TV commercials and magazine advertisements intended to sell drugs, denture adhesives, incontinence paraphernalia, mobility scooters, reverse mortgages, gold coins, disaster food, prepaid funerals and all the other products that older people can be scared into buying.

The seniors in these ads, having purchased these amazing products, are now free of care and worry. They can have fun! And almost always, the way they demonstrate how much fun they are having in their suddenly carefree lives is by . . . grinning. That's pretty much it. Sometimes they're grinning on a golf course, sometimes on a beach. Sometimes they're a grinning couple; sometimes there are seven or eight of them, all grinning like maniacs. It's never clear *why* they're grinning: nothing amusing appears to be happening. In fact, nothing of any kind is happening, other than a bunch of old people standing around grinning. They're having senior fun!

But it doesn't look like *real* fun, at least not to my eyes. I believe real fun needs to have an element of the unexpected, of adventure, maybe some weirdness, maybe some risk, possibly an arrest. I'd like to see a senior-citizen-product TV commercial in which the seniors, having just discovered, let's say, an amazing breakthrough laxative, are celebrating their emancipation from constipation by—I'm just spitballing here—blowing up a toilet with military-grade explosives. Maybe in the background there's a bong. THAT would look like fun.

So how can older people like me keep having fun? In an effort to answer that question, I decided to take an inventory of the truly fun experiences I've had in the past couple of decades. Most of them, I concluded, involved traveling, especially with my family. I know not everyone is physically or financially capable of traveling. But if you are, I highly recommend it: travel forces you out of your routine and opens up opportunities to have adventures.

Not all travel adventures are fun, of course. Commercial air travel is often an adventure, but it's usually not the "Wow, this is amazing!" kind of adventure. It's more the "Wow, we missed our connecting flight so we'll be spending the night on hard airport chairs under TV monitors blaring CNN!" kind of adventure.[10] But if you somehow manage, despite the efforts of the airline industry, to actually reach your destination, travel adventures tend to be the good kind of fun.[11]

The most fun adventure my family ever had was a few years ago, when we traveled to a wildlife preserve called

---

10   It's a good thing they don't allow firearms in airports, because by now I definitely would have shot a CNN monitor.

11   This is assuming that your destination is not New York's LaGuardia Airport and Permanent Construction Hellzone, which is littered with the skeletons of travelers who died of starvation waiting for the correct shuttle bus.

Londolozi in South Africa. We flew there from Johannesburg in an alarmingly funky old prop plane, which had to circle the dirt airstrip while the staff chased away some animals so we could land. From there we were transported via an open Land Rover to the compound. It was surrounded by a high fence, with an opening for vehicles that had an electrified grate on the ground to keep animals out.

We were dropped off in front of the lodge, and as we stood there with our luggage, a large elephant suddenly appeared in the fence opening, maybe twenty yards from us. The elephant kept stepping on the electrified grate, backing off, then stepping on it again; he was clearly trying to get into where we were. There was nobody else around; basically it was just us and an elephant, which—this bears repeating—was quite large. Michelle expressed concern about this situation; I, assuming the traditional role of Man in Charge, assured her we had nothing to worry about, based on my extensive experience of never having been anywhere near Africa.

At that moment a lodge staff member came trotting up. I assumed he was going to confirm that we had nothing to worry about. Instead he said, "We need to get out of here right now," as he continued trotting past.

"What about our luggage?" asked Michelle.

"He doesn't want your luggage," said the staff person over his shoulder.

So we trotted hastily after him into the lodge. Seconds later, the elephant got through the gate. The staff told us that they called him Night Shift, because every night he tried to get into the compound. I asked if he was dangerous. The staff did not really answer, but their expressions said: "It's a wild animal the size of a bus. What do YOU think?"

That was definitely the most exciting check-in of my life.

At dinner we were given a safety briefing, the main point of which was that we were not, for any reason, EVER, to go outside at night unaccompanied. A staff member escorted us from the dining area back to our bungalow. He carried a large, powerful flashlight; he kept sweeping the beam around, peering into the darkness. He told us that we had to stay close together, and that if we encountered an animal, under no circumstances—he stressed this repeatedly—were we to run.

We asked what would happen if we ran.

He said: "If you run, we are all dead."

He did not appear to be joking.

We didn't see any animals on the way back to the bungalow, but Night Shift spent the night in our vicinity. We knew this because in the morning, when we went outside, we found a mound of poop the size of a Fiat on our doorstep. It was sort of like when you're staying in a hotel, and they give you a complimentary *USA Today*. Welcome to Africa!

Breakfast was also an adventure. We ate in an open-air dining area surrounded by trees that were occupied by a gang of monkeys with low ethical standards and a highly sophisticated understanding of geometry. They observed the diners closely, figuring the angles and the distances, and if you got an inch too far from your plate, BAM, a monkey would leap from a tree, dart across the table in a blur of fur, snatch a piece of your fruit and leap back into the tree, setting off an explosion of screeching commentary from the other monkeys ("Bob got an apple!" "Well done, Bob!").

Some of the dining-area staff carried slingshots and tried to keep the monkeys at bay by shooting pebbles at them. They almost always missed. In what was clearly an ongoing battle, the monkeys were winning.

After breakfast the real adventure began, as we rode around the savanna in an open Land Rover with two supremely skilled and knowledgeable guides, Alfred Mathebula and Bennet Mathose. Those guys could track a mosquito through a thunderstorm blindfolded. They showed us giraffes, elephants, rhinos, buffalo, warthogs, wildebeests, hyenas and many nervous deerlike critters that belong to various species but all fall into the zoological category of "lunch." We followed a leopard named Camp Pan as he patiently stalked an impala, which managed to get away, and thank God it did, because it looked like Bambi, only cuter. If Camp Pan had caught it, my daughter would still be sobbing. We saw a pair of naked hippopotamuses doing it, and let me just say that if you ever get a chance to witness this amazing natural event, you will feel (1) profound respect for female hippos as a gender, and (2) a powerful urge to poke out your own eyeballs.

Our Land Rover got incredibly close—I'm talking a few feet—to some lions, who during the day mainly lounge around looking badass. They didn't appear to be at all concerned about our presence, which makes sense. Their attitude was: "We're lions, and you are puny hairless sacks of meat."

Lying among the larger lions were some young ones, which looked very cute, almost cuddly.

"I want to hug one!" exclaimed my daughter-in-law, Laura, from the back seat.

Bennet, without turning around, said: "We will come back in the morning and fetch your shoes."

He also did not appear to be joking.

We went on a nighttime ride, during which Alfred and Bennet stopped out on the savanna and, after checking around for lions, let us get out of the Land Rover. We then had cocktails under a billion trillion stars, which is the best way to have cocktails. While we were standing there, a group of hyenas—which is technically known as a "cackle"[12]—came trotting directly toward us. This alarmed me. Hyenas look menacing enough in daylight, and downright scary when they're coming your way at night. I asked Bennet if we should maybe get back into the Land Rover. He shook his head.

"It is not always about us," he said.

And it wasn't about us. The hyenas trotted right past, ignoring us, except for one, who went directly to Bennet, stopped, sniffed him, then went trotting off after the cackle.

"He knows me," said Bennet.

---

12   Really. Look it up.

That's another great thing about travel: It often serves to remind you that the world is full of things that are not about you. Unless of course you're traveling via cruise ship, in which case *everything* is about you—feeding you, entertaining you, selling things to you, taking you on guided tours—which is why cruises, although they can be pleasant, are not, to my mind, nearly as much fun as the kind of traveling where you don't always know what will happen next.

So what I'm saying to you, especially if you're getting up in years, is: Don't settle for contentment. Don't just stand around grinning. *Get out there.* It's a wonderful world.

Even if you can't travel, you can still find ways to have genuine fun. The key, I think, is to stretch your boundaries, to escape the numbing routine that old age so easily decays into, to take a chance, get out of your comfort zone, maybe risk making a fool of yourself. When I inventoried my life, I concluded that, aside from traveling, most of the truly fun moments I've had in the past couple of decades have resulted from my involvement in two organizations—I use this term loosely—that are fundamentally ridiculous.

One of these organizations is the Lawn Rangers—or, as they are referred to in their press releases and basically nowhere else, the World Famous Lawn Rangers. This is a marching unit that performs precision lawn mower–and–broom routines in parades. (I am using "precision" in the sense of "not even remotely precise.") The Rangers are based out of the small Illinois town of Arcola, which bills itself as the Broom Corn Capital of the World, because at one time it produced corn used to make broom bristles. Arcola celebrates this proud heritage every year by holding the Broom Corn Festival, which features many exciting elements, including:

- A sweeping contest, in which contestants must use a broom to maneuver several pounds of corn seed around some barriers and into a hole. As you can imagine, it gets pretty intense.
- Food, including pork chop on a stick.
- A beer tent.
- The largest gathering of porta-potties[13] in Central Illinois.

But the highlight of the Broom Corn Festival is the parade, and the highlight of the parade is the appear-

---

13   Technically known as a "trickle."

ance of the World Famous Lawn Rangers. I joined this crack unit back in 1992, at the invitation of one of its founders, Pat Monahan. I traveled to Arcola—located in Douglas County, the flattest county in Illinois—where I attended the Lawn Rangers' business meeting, at which the Rangers prepared for the parade via a strict regimen that included:

- Drinking beer.
- Listening to the team doctor's report, given by a Ranger who was not technically a doctor—technically, he worked at a hardware store—but did have a doctor-style bag containing an array of truly alarming sexual implements, which he displayed one by one, often introducing a new implement by saying, "I don't know if I should show you this one . . ."
- Drinking more beer.
- Watching talent demonstrations from various Rangers, including the legendary Doug Reeder, whose specialty is presenting original works of performance art involving the word "moon." At my first business meeting, he climbed a ladder and removed, one by one, approximately ten pairs of boxer shorts en route to a climactic finale that involved shooting a bottle rocket *out of his*

butt. It was one of the most impressive things I have ever seen a human do, and I have seen childbirth at close range. I missed an even more amazing finale, in which Ranger Reeder revealed that he had a potato gun between his thighs, from which he fired off a blast of chili. (At least everybody hoped it was chili.)

- Drinking some more beer.
- And maybe having a few more beers.

Another highlight of the business meeting is rookie orientation, during which veteran Rangers—wielding toilet plungers to denote their rank—train first-time Rangers to execute the precision maneuvers that will be used in the parade.

Each Ranger marches holding a broom in one hand and pushing a lawn mower with the other. Some of the lawn mowers are "show mowers," which have been customized by the addition of some decorative object such as a stuffed animal, easy chair, plastic snowman, commode, etc. Rangers wear cowboy hats, and sometimes black masks to protect our secret identities; we also wear aprons with pockets containing candies that we toss to the crowd, or, if we get hungry, eat.

At various points along the parade route, the leaders will hoist their plungers and give the "Brooms up!" command—signaling the Rangers to raise their brooms— followed by a command to execute one of the two precision maneuvers:

1. "Walk the Dog," in which the Rangers run around in small circles, turning their mowers 360 degrees, then resume marching in approximately the original direction.

2. "Cross and Toss," in which the Rangers—who march in two columns—switch places with the Rangers across from them, and then toss their brooms to each other, and then sometimes pick the brooms up off the ground because they failed to catch them. (This is a result of the beer part of the business meeting.)

Now, I know what you're thinking. You're thinking: *Grown men are doing this? Isn't that kind of immature?*

No! It is not "kind of" immature. It is *extremely* immature.[14] The truth is that the Rangers venture far beyond the realm of immature, deep into stupid territory.

---

14   In fact the official Ranger motto is "You're only young once, but you can always be immature."

But guess what? We have *fun*. And the spectators love us. Part of their enjoyment, I believe, derives from knowing that, no matter what kind of idiotic behavior they may have engaged in, they have never looked as ridiculous as we do. But mainly they love us because the Lawn Rangers—I reiterate—are FUN.

And for idiots having fun, the Rangers have some pretty impressive accomplishments. They've marched in parades all over the country, including in the Rose Bowl and Fiesta Bowl parades. They've also marched in Chicago's St. Patrick's Day parade. It was there, in 2003, that a young, up-and-coming Illinois politician named Barack Obama, campaigning for the US Senate, stopped to meet the Rangers, and—showing the kind of instinct for the dramatic gesture that characterizes born leaders—posed for a picture brandishing a toilet plunger over his head.

Five years later, Obama was elected president of the United States. Whether this was a direct result of his Ranger encounter, nobody can say. But consider this: after Obama was elected, Pat Monahan applied to have the Lawn Rangers march in his inaugural parade, and, incredibly, *we were accepted*. I am not making this up.

And so it was that on January 20, 2009, amid the fifteen thousand participants in the inaugural parade—

which included numerous marching bands and military units, wearing pristine uniforms and stepping in perfect unison—there were fifty-one Lawn Rangers, and I am proud to say I was one of them. We wore our hats and masks, of course, but in recognition of the majesty of the occasion, we also wore bright-red polyester graduation gowns.[15] We had a nice selection of show mowers, including one with a large reproduction of the photo of Obama holding the plunger. My mower had a miniature bed on it, and a sign that said, EMBEDDED REPORTER.

Also with us were five women wearing fake beards and dressed vaguely like famous deceased Illinois person Abraham Lincoln. They marched in front of the Ranger unit carrying a banner informing the spectators that we were World Famous.

We were slotted toward the end of the parade, so we spent a long, cold day waiting in outdoor holding areas with the other marching units and a small, brave, badly outmanned band of porta-potties that I imagine had to be destroyed later by cruise missiles.

Finally, with night falling and temperatures dropping,

---

15 Supplied by the Collegiate Cap & Gown Co., proudly located in Arcola.

the Rangers got the signal to march. We rolled our show mowers onto Pennsylvania Avenue, holding our brooms high. At that point the huge crowds had left and only a few smallish clots of spectators were still spectating, but we performed our precision maneuvers for them, and were almost rewarded with an appreciative "Huh?"

Finally the brightly lit reviewing stand in front of the White House came into view ahead. By then it was mostly empty, and I assumed all the big-name dignitaries were long gone. But as we drew close, we saw them, watching us from behind the bulletproof glass just a few feet away: President and Michelle Obama, and Vice President Joe Biden. At first they looked puzzled—not a surprising reaction, as we were surely the only unit in the parade boasting a lawn mower with a toilet mounted on it—but then the president saw the picture of himself holding the plunger aloft. He said something to the First Lady, and they both burst out laughing.

Then we Rangers performed a precision maneuver. If I recall correctly, it was "Walk the Dog."

And then we moved past the reviewing stand, and our parade was over.

But *damn*, that was fun.

That was also the last time I marched with the Rangers. Every year, Pat Monahan sends me an email reminding me that the Broom Corn Festival is coming up, and the Rangers will be meeting and marching. Every year I've been too busy to go.

And every year I get another year older.

I need to reconnect with the Rangers. I need a fix of stupid, immature fun.

Which brings me to the other fundamentally ridiculous organization that I've been involved with: the Rock Bottom Remainders. This is a rock band of authors that was founded by Kathi Goldmark, a smart, funny, warm and joyful woman who was *always* up for fun. (She carried kazoos in her purse, because, hey, you never know when you'll need a kazoo.)

In 1992, Kathi, who ran a company that escorted book-touring authors around San Francisco, had the idea of bringing a bunch of writers together to raise money for a worthy cause. Basically she invited every author she knew, and the ones who said yes, regardless of talent, formed the band. Among the original authors were Amy Tan, Stephen King, Ridley Pearson, Roy Blount Jr., Barbara Kingsolver, Tad Bartimus, Robert Fulghum, Matt Groening, Greil Marcus, Joel Selvin, Dave Marsh and me. We had a professional drummer, Josh Kelly, and Kathi somehow recruited an actual rock legend, Al Kooper, to be our musical director.

The plan was for the Remainders to perform for one night, then disband. From a strictly musical standpoint, we *should* have disbanded, because we were terrible. Roy Blount described our musical genre as "hard listening." We played music by what I call the Rumor Method, wherein from time to time an alarming rumor went around the band: *There might have been a chord change.* This prompted everybody to change to a new chord. Although not necessarily the *same* new chord.

So we did not show musical promise, in that first performance. But we had *way* too much fun to want to stop.

As Amy Tan put it: "I would do this to kill the whales."

And as Steve King put it: "We ain't done yet."

And so the Remainders kept going. We developed a repertoire of onstage shtick and hijinks to compensate for our musical inadequacy; our goal was to entertain rather than impress, and we generally succeeded, especially if the audience was drinking. We wound up playing for more than twenty years, almost always for book-related or benefit events.

Along the way some people dropped out of the band, and others participated less frequently. But new authors joined us, including Mitch Albom, Scott Turow, Greg Iles, James McBride, Frank McCourt, my brother Sam Barry, Alan Zweibel, Mary Karr and dozens of guest authors. We acquired a saxophonist, Erasmo Paolo, and a manager/impresario, Ted Habte-Gabr, who could schmooze a turtle out of its shell.

Occasionally real big-time musicians performed with the Remainders, including Bruce Springsteen,[16] Judy Collins, Monte Montgomery, Lesley Gore, Nestor Torres, Darlene Love and Gloria Gaynor. Warren Zevon performed with us for years; he was succeeded as a regular guest star by Roger McGuinn, one of the founders of the Byrds.

Musically, the Remainders got a little better over the years, although we didn't get anywhere near good. But it was never really about the music. We had become friends—real friends, the kind you turn to for comfort when things are bad, and to celebrate with when things are good. This will sound corny, but it's true: we became family. In fact one of the things we celebrated was the marriage of Kathi and my brother Sam, who met because of the band.

---

16   After performing with the Remainders, Springsteen told us: "Don't get any better, or you'll just be another lousy garage band."

So we kept playing, year after year, because we loved to hang out together. And because we had fun. *Man,* did we have fun. To cite just a few memories:

There was the night in Cleveland when, after playing a benefit show at the Rock and Roll Hall of Fame, we gathered in somebody's hotel room, where some band members got to singing Irish folk songs with such spirit that a hotel security guy came and pounded on our door. And thus we got to enjoy the spectacle of the security guy delivering a stern keep-it-down lecture to two contrite individuals: Roger McGuinn, who is *in* the Rock and Roll Hall of Fame, and his fellow Irishman Pulitzer Prize–winner Frank McCourt.

There was the night in Nashville when Steve King was singing "Teen Angel," and a woman in the crowd in front of him raised her arms to reveal that—apparently this was meant as a tribute—*all her fingernails were on fire.* I still don't know how she did that. I do know that I agreed with Ridley when, looking at the woman looking at Steve, he said, "I don't ever want to be that famous."

There was the night in Miami when Carl Hiaasen performed with us as a guitarist. Carl is a wonderfully talented writer but—I say this as a friend—he is musically challenged, even by Remainders standards. He'd been taking guitar lessons to prepare for his performance with us, but he was still very nervous.

> Q. How nervous was he?
> A. He was so nervous that *he brought his guitar teacher onstage with him.*

Really. The two of them stood together at the back of the stage, with their amplifiers adjacent to each other, and all night long we could hear the teacher yelling the chords to Carl ("E! A! NOW BACK TO E!") while Carl tried frantically, with varying degrees of success, to locate each new chord before the teacher yelled another one at him. This was highly entertaining to listen to, and I can't say that it noticeably impacted our overall sound.

There was the time in Washington, DC, when Amy Tan had brought along a portable karaoke device, which graded you, using a scale of zero to 100, on how close your singing was to the original record. We got Roger McGuinn to sing along to the Byrds' classic recording of "Turn! Turn! Turn!," in which the lead singer is: Roger McGuinn. The machine gave Roger a 96, so he tried again, and got a 97. So he tried *again*, but he only got to

98. We told him he was a pretty good singer, but he was no Roger McGuinn.

There was the time—I don't remember the city—when we almost performed "Wild Thing" correctly. "Wild Thing" is one of the simplest garage-rock songs there is; it requires almost no musical talent. But we never got it right, and without naming any names I would have to say that the problem was Roy Blount.

Roy's role in "Wild Thing" was to deliver the line "You MOVE me." The problem was that he could never get the timing right: he was always early or late. (By way of background: Roy is the founder and national chairman of the League of the Singing Impaired.) Roy's timing got to be a running joke in the band, to the point where, unbeknownst to him, we made a mass bet on whether he'd deliver his line too soon or too late. That night, with several hundred dollars on the line, the critical moment came; all of us turned to look at Roy, and he, incredibly, for the first and only time, delivered the line *exactly right*. Unfortunately, this caused the rest of us to collapse in laughter and thus totally screw up the song. Thus our record of being the only rock band in the world never to perform "Wild Thing" correctly remained intact.

And there was the night in New York when we performed our extremely campy version of "Leader of the Pack," in which lead singer Amy Tan plays the young woman whose parents make her dump the motorcycle-gang leader she loves, and he dies in a tragic crash. Amy's husband, Lou DeMattei, who in real life is a tax lawyer, played the part of the Leader of the Pack. He wore a leather jacket and pretended to be driving a motorcycle; he simulated the crash by diving dramatically onto the stage, where he writhed around in simulated agony, much to the enjoyment of the crowd. Seeking to add to the merriment, Steve King and I started kicking him, causing him to writhe even more as he crawled off the stage. Ha ha! What fun!

As it turned out, Lou was not having nearly as much fun as we were. After the show, we learned that he'd been taken to the hospital, where he was diagnosed with a broken collarbone. So when Steve and I were kicking him, he'd been writhing in actual, nonsimulated agony. Needless to say we felt terrible, although Lou was a great sport; he remained on the band's multicity tour and continued to play the Leader of the Pack, although he wore a sling and no longer dived onto the stage. So he was more like the Leader of the Walking Wounded.

I also had an alarming band-related medical incident,

after a performance on a different night in New York. The band had retired to our hotel bar, where I ended up sitting between Roy Blount and Scott Turow. Both of them were telling stories, and I found myself trying to listen to both of them, switching back and forth. I also found myself drinking a number[17] of vodka gimlets.

Scott's story involved his spleen, and it was long and complicated. Between the switching back and forth and the gimlets, I became confused, so I interrupted him and said, "Wait, do you have a spleen or not?"

"I don't," said Scott patiently. "That's the point."

So he resumed telling the story, and I resumed switching back and forth. A little while and a gimlet or two later, while listening to Scott, I again became confused, so I interrupted him and said, "Wait . . . So you *do* have a spleen?"

Scott again explained, a little less patiently, that he did not have a spleen.

If you have ever spent any time in the company of a drunken idiot, you will not be surprised to learn that, a little while later, I *again* became confused and inquired as to Scott's current status, spleenwise. This time, in-

---

17   Possibly six.

stead of answering, he took a Sharpie and wrote NO SPLEEN in large letters on my right forearm. That solved my retention problem, and the rest of the evening passed without incident as far as I can remember, which is not very far.

The next morning the band had to catch an early train to Boston. I woke up in my hotel room in extremely poor condition and staggered toward the toilet. En route, I caught sight of my reflection in the bathroom mirror and realized that *something was written on my arm.*

I looked down and read the words.

NO SPLEEN.

For a few terrifying seconds, my brain—which, in its defense, had the same level of neural functionality as a Bermuda onion—could come up with only one explanation. You know that urban legend where the traveling businessman is drugged and wakes up in a hotel bathtub packed with ice, and he sees a note telling him that one of his kidneys has been harvested? I thought that was what had happened to me, except instead of kidney harvesters, *I was the victim of spleen harvesters.*

I started frantically checking myself for an incision, which was problematic because I don't know where my spleen is. Then, as my brain rebooted, it occurred to me that the spleen is not an organ with strong resale value. You never hear about anybody urgently awaiting a spleen donor. Surgeons routinely remove spleens and throw them away. It would be moronic to harvest one. "He's so stupid he'd harvest a spleen" is probably a common insult in organ-harvesting circles.

After a few seconds I remembered that Scott had written the words on my arm, and I had a subdued yet painful laugh at my own expense, then continued staggering toward the toilet.

But those were an exciting few seconds.

These are just some of the many fond memories I have of being part of the Remainders. We had a wonderful run, lasting way longer than any of us expected. But over the years, time—in this one respect, we were exactly like the Beatles—took its toll on the band.

Warren Zevon died in 2003.

Frank McCourt died in 2009.

And then in 2012, Kathi Goldmark, the woman who brought us all together, the heart and soul of the band, reached the end of a brutal battle with breast cancer. At the time the Remainders were booked to play two shows in California. Kathi, who *never* missed a Remainders gig, hoped to hang on long enough to be there. When she realized she wasn't going to make it, she told my brother she wanted the Remainders to play anyway.

And so we did. In both shows, we stopped in the middle and did a tribute to Kathi, ending it by performing a wonderfully funny song she wrote, "Older Than Him." It's a country/western ballad about a middle-aged woman—that would be Kathi—who's sitting in a bar when a young studly male walks in. She tries to attract his attention, but he doesn't even know she exists.

The chorus goes:

Oh, I wonder if he'd care
If he knew I had underwear
Older than him
Better get back to the gym.

On both nights, that song brought down the house. One last ovation for Kathi.

We thought those would be our last shows. We told the press we were disbanding, and we believed it. We'd lost our founder, and we were getting older, maybe too old to be putting on wigs and blowing kazoos and prancing around like fools making mediocre music.

But we missed each other. And we missed the fun.

And we're a terrible band, so it only makes sense that we would be terrible at disbanding. In 2015, we were invited to play at the Tucson Festival of Books. Most of us said yes, and we played to a big, enthusiastic crowd, and it felt wonderful, being together again. A few months later, we played at the Miami Book Fair; there was a monsoon that night, and we ended up having to move into a small-ish tent, but we still had a blast.

That was the last time we played. As I write these words, I don't know if we'll ever play again. Getting the band together is a logistical and financial hassle, and the truth is, there's a limited demand for our musical talents. So maybe we're really done this time.

And maybe we should be. Maybe we're too old for this silliness.

But I don't want to quit. I want to believe that if my old dog can still have fun, I can, too. I don't want to wait until it's too late. I want to heed the words of my friend and bandmate Warren Zevon. After Warren was diagnosed with terminal cancer, he went on David Letterman's show, and Letterman asked him how his approach to life had changed. This was Warren's answer:

"You know, you put more value on every minute . . . I mean, I always thought I kind of did that. I really always enjoyed myself. But it's more valuable now. You're reminded to enjoy every sandwich, and every minute of playing with the guys, and being with the kids and everything."

I don't, thank God, have terminal cancer. But I don't have forever, either. You get only so much time, and as Warren said, it's more valuable now. So I'm going to see if my bandmates, my friends, would be up for un-disbanding again, and making some more memories while we still can. I don't know if they'll be up for it. But I'm going to try.

I'm also going to reconnect with my Arcola roots. I sent an email to Pat Monahan, asking him when the World Famous Lawn Rangers will be marching next. He got right back to me: there's a Broom Corn Festival coming up. I plan to be there, pushing my show mower and performing highly imprecise precision maneuvers. I plan to have some *fun*.

It's more valuable now.

THE THIRD LESSON FROM LUCY

I was one of the last people to find out about "mind-fulness." By the time I'd heard of it, major corporations and government agencies were putting their employees through mindfulness training. I did not view this as a positive sign. In my experience, any trend that reaches the point where large organizations are inflicting it on their personnel has a high statistical probability of being stupid.

A good example is "diversity training." This is a process whereby a corporation makes a group of employees sit in a room with a professional diversity trainer, who subjects them to lectures, videos and role-playing exercises about the importance of respecting each other until the employees finally come to the realization that they hate the diversity trainer and want to do the diametrical opposite of whatever he or she is telling them.

I've been subjected to diversity training several times, and every time the trainer treated us employees like exceptionally dull-witted six-year-olds, unable to grasp how racist and sexist and generally wrong-thinking we were. This is not a good way to win people over. Of course we all *said* the right things in diversity class, because compliance was mandatory and we wanted to get out of there. But inside we were seething. We were ready to go out and join the Klan. *Even the black employees.* That's how resentful we were.

No, that's a joke. I apologize if it offends you. But that brings me to another thing I hated about diversity training: the trainers insisted that if anybody is offended by something you say, you are automatically wrong. The problem with that is, there are people who are offended by *everything*. Being offended is their primary reason for existing. If you let them decide what you can and cannot say, they will suck all the humor out of the world.

I am an expert on this topic. In my humor-columnist career I wrote tens of thousands of jokes, and, based on the mail I received, I believe that *every single joke* offended somebody. For example, I once wrote that "Hoosier" is a stupid nickname for Indianans to call themselves because nobody seems to know for sure what it means. "For all we know," I wrote, "'Hoosier' could be a Native American word for 'has sex with caribou.'"

This joke was deeply offensive to many Hoosiers, who wrote me angry letters informing me in no uncertain terms that everybody knows *exactly* what "Hoosier" means, and then proceeded to provide several dozen completely different definitions. My favorite letter came from an offended Hoosier who wrote: "Indiana has no caribou." Case closed!

My point is that diversity training, at least in my experience, is annoying and counterproductive. Yet corporations continue to push it, just as they continue to hold "team-building" and "bonding" exercises, wherein employees are required to go on "retreats" and participate in "adventures" such as whitewater rafting, rock climbing, bear wrestling and worm grunting. The idea is that these employees develop a bond of mutual trust based on not ratting each other out to management when they sneak away from the retreat and go to a bar.

My favorite example of insane things that corporations do to innocent employees involves Burger King, which, in 2001, held a motivational event for employees of the marketing department. (Whenever you see the word "motivational" used in a corporate-training context, you should mentally substitute the word "stupid.") At this event, Burger King had its employees, under the guidance of a paid consultant, break boards, smash bricks, walk on sharp nails and bend steel bars with their throats. So far, so good. These are all skills that are no doubt invaluable in the modern corporate marketing environment.

But then things got really motivational. Before I tell you what happened, let's review what sort of corporation Burger King is. It is the sort of corporation that sells hamburgers. Its very name makes reference to this fact. Burger King sells more than *two billion hamburgers* a year. And what is a hamburger? A hamburger is cooked cow meat. You would think that management personnel at Burger King—even in the marketing department—would be aware of the consequences of exposing flesh to very high temperatures.

So what do you suppose the Burger King employees did, as the culmination of their motivational event? I will tell you, using capital letters for emphasis: THEY WALKED BAREFOOT ACROSS HOT COALS.

This is called fire walking, and it is a "confidence-building" exercise that has been popularized by such leading motivators as Tony Robbins, who is so motivational my head hurts just from thinking about him.

Now, if you try to make a three-year-old child, or a dog, or for that matter a spider, walk barefoot across hot coals, that child or dog or spider will refuse. But your modern corporate employee, eager to remain employed, can be coerced into doing pretty much anything, as evidenced by the fact that one hundred Burger King employees took off their shoes and socks and walked barefoot across what the *Miami Herald* later described as "an eight-foot strip of glowing, white-hot coals."

What could possibly go wrong? Nothing! Unless you count the fact that—to quote the *Herald* again—"about a dozen Burger King employees suffered at least first- and second-degree burns on their feet." One woman went to the hospital. Several people were in such pain that they needed wheelchairs.

Does that mean that the fire walking was a bad idea? Not in the objective opinion of the consultant who was paid to organize it! He told the *Herald*: "The majority of the people get through it without a nick or a blister. When you see over 100 people and only 10 to 15 people have blisters, I don't term that unusual."

He also said—this is an actual quote, and it may well

be the greatest statement ever emitted by a consultant—
"Some people just have incredibly sensitive feet."

A Burger King marketing vice president who was involved in organizing the event, and who was among
those injured, agreed that the fire walking was a swell
idea. She told the *Herald*—this is an excellent example of
the marketing mind at work—"It was a great experience
for everyone."

No doubt it was! I bet the participants felt a new
sense of confidence as they walked out of the event, or,
in the case of those with incredibly sensitive feet, were
rolled out.

My point is, I am highly skeptical of any trend that
large corporations participate in. And so when I heard
about mindfulness, I assumed it was just another waste
of time. But I kept hearing about it and hearing about it,
until finally I took the unusual (for me) step of actually
finding out what it is using professional journalism techniques, by which I mean Google.

As I understand it, mindfulness basically means being
fully in the present moment—not rehashing and second-
guessing the past, not fretting about the future, but focus-
ing on *right now.* It means being aware of your physical
sensations, your feelings, your thoughts. It also means

accepting these thoughts and feelings, without judging whether they're right or wrong. It means not overthinking everything.

Mindfulness, according to its advocates, makes you more relaxed, more at peace. Mindfulness training, which includes meditation techniques, is said by many to reduce stress and make you healthier and happier.

So mindfulness sounds like a pretty good idea.

You know who's really mindful, in her own way?

Lucy.

She is *always* in the present moment. She lives for now. She doesn't dwell on the past or worry about the future. She definitely doesn't overthink. She spends most of the day in a serene, semimeditative state that I would call Dog Snooze, but she's always aware of what's going on around her, and the instant anything happens she is *right there*, totally into whatever it is, intensely aware of the sounds, the sights and of course the smells.

She accepts her feelings; she does not second-guess herself. Sometimes these are not happy feelings: for example, when the man comes to take our garbage, Lucy objects vociferously, because—she cannot believe we allow this to happen—he is *taking our garbage*. But the instant the man is gone from our driveway, he's gone from Lucy's mind, and she's on to the next moment, which usually means back into Dog Snooze. She does not stress, and I envy that.

But what I really admire about Lucy's mindfulness—and here we are getting to the lesson for this chapter—is the way it enables her to be such a wonderful companion. It's a cliché, but only because it's so obviously true: *nobody loves you the way your dog loves you.* When you're with your dog, you may mentally be elsewhere, but your dog is not; your dog is always right there with you. When you're gone, your dog is waiting for you to come back, so it can be with you again. Because being with you makes your dog happier than anything else.

I spend most working days at home, and Lucy is always close, moving from room to room as I do, waiting to see where I settle and then finding a spot on the floor a few feet away. When I walk in her direction, her tail thumps the floor, a Geiger counter of happiness. When I pet her, her entire body quivers with joy. When I talk to her, she listens to me as hard as she can, staring at me intently, head cocked, ears flexed, eager to pick up every sound, especially if one of the sounds turns out to be "chicken."

She's not just near me; she's *with* me. And being with

me makes her happy. It's the simple pleasure of being in the moment with somebody you love.

You know who rarely experiences this pleasure?

Me.

I'm often with people I love, but I'm rarely in the moment. I'm checking my phone—even though I checked it fifteen seconds ago—or I'm thinking about things that have nothing to do with the moment. Most of the time these are not significant or pressing thoughts, but my brain insists on thinking them anyway. This means I'm often distracted, which makes me a lousy companion.

It can also lead to awkward situations. Let's say I'm sitting at the breakfast table with Michelle, and we're theoretically having a conversation. But my brain has decided to think about something else. This means that my mouth, which is not the brightest organ in my body, has to fend for itself as it attempts to hold up its end of the conversation without really knowing what it's talking about:

MICHELLE: So I'm worried about her.

MY MOUTH: Yeah.

MY BRAIN (*to itself*): *The new season of* The Walking Dead *starts tonight.*

MICHELLE: I mean, why would she say that?

MY MOUTH: Right.

MY BRAIN: *I definitely want to record that.*

MICHELLE: She never said anything like that before, at least not to me.

MY MOUTH: Hm.

MY BRAIN: *I recorded last season, so maybe it will automatically record this season.*

MICHELLE: Do you think she means it?

MY MOUTH: Huh.

MY BRAIN: *I should check the DVR.*

MICHELLE: What?

MY MOUTH: Right.

MY BRAIN: *I need to make sure it's recording the high-def version.*

MICHELLE: Does that mean you think she means it?

MY MOUTH: Hm.

MY BRAIN: *There's definitely a difference between high def and regular def.*

MICHELLE: Hello? Are you listening to me?

(At this point, my mouth, sensing that it's in trouble, sends an urgent back-channel message via my nervous system to my brain.)

MY MOUTH: *MAYDAY MAYDAY MAYDAY*

MY BRAIN: *What?*

MY MOUTH: *She wants to know if we're listening to her!*

MY BRAIN: *What is she talking about?*

MY MOUTH: *I don't know!*

MY BRAIN: *Well THINK, damn it!*

MY MOUTH: *I can't! I'm a mouth!*

MY BRAIN: *Now we're in trouble, you asshole!*

MY ASSHOLE: *Hey! Leave me out of this!*

MICHELLE: Did you just fart?

I do this all the time,[18] and not just with Michelle. I can be in the midst of a group of people having a conversation, and I will appear to be fully engaged—my eyes tracking from speaker to speaker, my head nodding at appropriate times, my mouth smiling when it senses that somebody has said something amusing—and I will have *absolutely no idea* what they're talking about. This would not be so bad if my brain were curing cancer or writing the great American novel. But my brain is almost always thinking about something unimportant or actively stupid.

Which means I spend a lot of time effectively ignoring

---

18   I don't mean that I fart all the time. Perhaps I do, but that's not what I mean.

people. Time after time I miss out, for no good reason, on the simple pleasure of human companionship. And when the people I'm ignoring are the people I love, I deprive myself of the greatest source of happiness in my life.

As if I have something better to do.

I'm a fool.

This leads us to the third Lesson from Lucy:

Pay Attention to the People You Love.
(Not Later. Right Now.)

This is another one of those obvious truths that you re-discover every time somebody you know dies. You think about the times you passed up chances to talk to or be with the person. You wish you could have those chances back. You vow not to make the same mistake with family and friends who are still alive. And maybe for a little while, you keep that vow. But sooner or later—usually sooner—you're back to paying way more attention to your phone than your loved ones. You're the same hyper-distracted work android you were before.

Until the next funeral.

And so on, rinse and repeat, until the funeral is yours,

and they bury you with your phone because God forbid you should miss an important text.

This depressing train of thought caused me to stop writing this chapter and call up an old friend, Mike Peters. Mike is a cartoonist. He won a Pulitzer Prize for his editorial cartoons, and he draws the syndicated comic strip *Mother Goose and Grimm*. He is also—and I do not believe this is an exaggeration—the sweetest man in the world. He makes the Dalai Lama look like Pol Pot. If a golden retriever were to be transformed into a human being, that golden retriever would be Mike Peters. When he meets new people, he is so excited, so *joyful*, that they often think he's faking it.

"He's not faking it!" I tell these people, as Mike is hugging them. "He's really like this!"

Here are two more things you should know about Mike:

1. He has, over the course of his life, owned *seven* Superman costumes.[19]

---

19 His mom gave him his first Superman costume for Christmas when he was eight. Mike recalls: "I felt like it was the Shroud of Turin. I couldn't put it on so I took it up to my room and hung it in my closet and I just

2. He is the happiest grown-up I know.

I got to know Mike through a mutual friend, the great cartoonist Jeff MacNelly. Jeff was prodigiously talented: among many other honors, he won three Pulitzers for his editorial cartoons; he also drew the popular *Shoe* strip. He was a hugely entertaining person—a big, outdoorsy, up-for-fun guy with a booming laugh and a hilariously subversive mind. He would have been welcome on the Washington cocktails-and-dinner circuit, but he was much happier on his farm, driving his pickup through mud puddles.

In addition to his other work, Jeff illustrated my humor column for a bunch of newspapers. Over the years, and over many beers, we became good friends. Jeff was a joy to collaborate with. Sometimes I'd be late on a column, and he'd call me up and ask me what it was about so he

---

sat there that Christmas and just looked at it. I put it on a couple of times but I didn't want it to get dirty. I would look out my window and wait for someone to do something wrong. I remember someone dropped a cup out their car window so I put on my Superman suit, ran down to my front porch and then flew over to the cup, picked it up and then flew back to my house and put the cup into the trash. Then I ran back to my room, took off the suit, hung it safely in the closet and waited for the next time to use it."

could get started on his drawing, and I'd say something vague, like, "It's about this guy who was sitting on a toilet and he got bit in the balls by a snake." And Jeff would say, "What kind of snake?" And I'd say, "A cobra." And Jeff would say, "OK," then hang up and produce a brilliant cartoon, much funnier than my column.

In 1999 Jeff called me and told me he'd been diagnosed with lymphoma. I said the usual inadequate oh-man-I'm-so-sorry things, but Jeff refused to let either one of us be depressed.

"They tell me that if you have to get cancer, this is the best kind," he said. "So I guess I should be pretty excited!" Then he laughed that big, booming laugh.

If there was humor to be found in a situation, Jeff would find it.

He died in less than a year. He worked right up to the end, drawing his cartoons from a bed in the Johns Hopkins Hospital.

His funeral was held near his farm in Virginia. A few months later, a bunch of us gathered for another smaller ceremony in Key West, a place Jeff loved. His wife, Susie, had a container of his ashes, and the plan was to go out on a sailboat—Jeff loved boats—and shoot his ashes out of a cannon. Jeff would have appreciated that.

So that's what we did. Some words were said, and Jeff's ashes were blasted out over the Atlantic with a satisfying boom, and everybody had a good cry, and some good laughs and some champagne.

On the way back to the dock, I sat on the deck next to Mike Peters, the two of us looking out at the water and talking about Jeff. Mike was Jeff's closest friend; he was with him in the hospital at the end, which was pretty rough. Mike told me that, as hospital staff came around, he found himself trying to make sure they really understood who Jeff was—that he was not just another patient, but a famous, award-winning cartoonist. When Mike tried to explain this, the staff people responded, "Oh yes, we know, this is Mr. MacNelly." In other words, they knew that was his name. Of course that's not what Mike meant; he wanted them to know *who Jeff was*, to appreciate him, his achievements, his fame, all his honors. His career.

But the medical staff didn't have time to appreciate Jeff's career. They were—understandably—focused on doing their jobs. To them Jeff *was* just another patient to be cared for before they moved on to the next patient, and the next. Jeff was a name on a chart.

Mr. MacNelly.

Mike said he thought about this, as he watched his best friend dying, and he realized something: *In the end, all that really matters—all you really have—is the people you love. Not your job, not your career, not your awards, not your money, not your stuff. Just your people.*

I asked Mike if this realization had changed him in any way. He said it had. Before, he said, if he was working and his wife or kids wanted to talk to him, he'd half-listen, but he'd keep holding his pen and looking at his drawing, sending the message: *I'm busy. This isn't your time. I have work to do.* But now, he said, he made himself put down his pen, turn away from his drawing, look the other person in the eyes and *listen*. And he'd keep listening for however long it took. And if that meant his work had to wait, that was OK.

"And you're still doing that?" I said. (Remember, this was months after Jeff's funeral.)

"I am," he said.

That conversation took place more than fifteen years ago, but I think about it every time some tragedy jolts me out of dithering about the distractions in my life and forces me to focus, if only briefly, on the people who actually make my life worthwhile. So when I was writing this chapter, I decided to call Mike, to see if (a) he remembered our conversation, and (b) he was still putting down his pen when his loved ones interrupted his work.

He said yes, absolutely, to both. These days the interrupters tend to be his grandkids, and instead of wanting to talk, they want him to jump with them on the trampoline. But he still puts down his pen, and he gets up and jumps.

So to summarize:

1. Lucy spends every second she can being as close as she can be to the people she loves. This makes her a happy dog.
2. Mike Peters, who is a busy guy facing constant deadlines, still makes a point of making time for, and jumping on the trampoline with, the people he loves. And he is the happiest person I know over the age of three.

These two happy souls are, by example, teaching an important lesson. And I'm trying to learn it. I've been making a conscious effort to focus on the people I'm with, especially my loved ones, and keep my phone in my pocket. This is not always easy. For one thing, sometimes my loved ones are looking at *their* phones. For another thing, my phone calls to me constantly.

"Dave!" it calls, from inside my pocket. "Oh Daa-ave! You haven't looked at Twitter for *nearly ninety seconds,* Dave! What if somebody just tweeted something? What if it's somebody *with a blue checkmark, Dave*? And *what about Facebook,* Dave? What if somebody you barely knew in high school fifty years ago has posted a hot political take or a photo of his or her dinner entrée AND YOU HAVE NOT SEEN IT YET, DAVE???"

It is strong, the call of the phone. But I can be stronger. I can be a better husband, a better dad, a better friend, a better—and happier—person. I can be mindful. I can stop wasting the dwindling minutes of the only life I'll ever have obsessing over past events I can't do anything about, and future events that might never happen. I can teach myself to focus on the only time that matters, which is *this moment right now*, and use this precious time to appreciate, to *cherish*, the people I love.

I really am going to do this.

Right after I check my phone.

THE FOURTH LESSON FROM LUCY

If I had to list the top five things that I am exceptionally good at, I'd go with, in no particular order:

- Sarcasm.
- Ridicule.
- Hand farts.
- Locating the bar at a wedding reception.
- Developing an instantaneous hatred for people I don't know.

It's the last one that I want to talk about in this chapter. I have a black belt in instantly hating strangers. Let's say you're at the front of a line of people waiting to buy ice cream, and I'm somewhere in the line behind you.

And let's say it's the kind of ice-cream shop where, if you ask, they'll give you a sample on a little tasting spoon so you can decide what flavor you want.

I'm OK with you getting a sample flavor. I'm even OK with you getting *two* sample flavors, even though, as I said, there's a line. So if you simply taste your samples and make your decision, you will not annoy me. OK, you will annoy me a little bit with the second sample, but not to the point of actual hatred.

But let's say that you're the kind of person who, knowing that people are waiting behind you, still takes thirty seconds or so to savor each sample—head cocked, lips smacking, as if you were tasting an expensive wine—and that you feel the need to share your opinions on each sample with your companions (you always have companions, who are also savoring multiple samples). And then, after your third or fourth sample, you frown thoughtfully, as though pondering a major financial transaction such as purchasing a house, and you turn from your companions to the harried employee waiting behind the counter, scoop in hand, for you to actually order something, and—as the line behind you lengthens—you say, "Let me try the coconut boysenberry rutabaga kale swirl again."

You need to know that I hate you. I don't care if you're taking a brief ice-cream break from your self-funded humanitarian mission to cure third-world orphans of horrible diseases: I hate you. If everybody else in the line hated you as much as I do, your body would burst into flames from the hate rays being beamed at it.

This is also how I feel about you if you wait until you get to the front of the line at a fast-food restaurant or movie-theater snack counter before you even *begin* your leisurely perusal of the menu, which has been posted prominently overhead the whole time.

Or if you drive your car past a long line of vehicles waiting to exit an expressway so you can butt in at the front.

Or if, when you stop for a red light, you immediately look down at your phone, and it apparently does not occur to you to glance up at the light from time to time in case for some reason—who knows, in this crazy world?—*it might turn green again*, which means that when it *does* turn green, to get you moving again, I—because I am *always* the driver behind you—have to honk, and in response you shoot me an annoyed glance in your rearview mirror, as if to say, *Can't you see I'm texting?*

Or if you talk so loudly into your mobile phone that

the rest of us can't avoid hearing your end of your conversation, which for the record is always inane.

Or if, at a concert or sports event, you repeatedly stand up when nobody else around you is standing up, so the people behind you—and I am *always* one of the people behind you—have to either stand up themselves or repeatedly ask you to sit down, which annoys you because in your mind standing up shows that you're a REAL fan, when in fact it shows that you're a jerk.

Or if you smoke your cigar where the rest of us have to smell it.

Or if you litter.

Or if you summon your waiter by snapping your fingers.

Or if you sit on your Harley in a crowded public space and repeatedly rev the stupidly loud engine for no apparent reason other than that you need attention.

Or if I am holding the door for you and you walk past me without so much as a glance, let alone a thank-you.

Or if you are giving a breakfast speech, and you begin by saying, "Good morning!" and the audience, which is trying to wake up, mumbles, "Good morning," and instead of starting your speech you say, "Come on, now! You can do better than that!" And you make the audience say, "Good morning" *again*, after which you say, "That's better!" with a big, self-satisfied grin, as if you are being original and clever, instead of hackneyed and irritating. *Just give your stupid speech and let us drink our coffee, OK?*

All of these behaviors, and many more—do not get me started on airline passengers—will cause me to hate complete strangers. I am capable of hating dozens of strangers in a single day. If I'm driving in Miami, surrounded by motorists who exhibit the same understanding of basic traffic laws as brain-damaged flatworms, I can hate dozens of complete strangers *per minute.*

At this point you may be thinking: *Whoa, Dave, you sound like you might have an anger problem there.*

No, I do not have an anger problem. I simply have a low tolerance for idiots and jerks, OK? So why don't you take your amateur long-distance psychoanalysis and *shove it up your . . .*

Sorry! OK, maybe you're right: I can be a pretty angry person. Although you would not know this from observing me. If you were the multiple-flavor-sampling jerk holding up the ice-cream line, and you happened to glance back at me, you would see what appears to be a calm, mild-mannered seventy-year-old man with a hairstyle popularized by the Beatles in 1964. You would have no way of knowing that I am fantasizing about watching you be lobotomized without anesthesia by an orangutan wielding an unsterilized tire iron.

This is because I almost always hide my rage from the person who is enraging me. I keep it bottled up inside, unless I am pushed to the breaking point by some extreme provocation. And when I say "some extreme provocation," I mean "customer service."

I will give you an example. One afternoon a few years back I was working at home—and when I say "working," I mean "not working per se, but looking at my computer"—when the Internet went out. Moments later Wilfredo tapped on the window. Wilfredo is the hardworking man who fights a courageous weekly battle to prevent the aggressive Florida vegetation comprising our "yard" from getting inside our house and killing us all in a savage outburst of photosynthesis. Wilfredo told me, very apologetically, that while trimming some bushes he had accidentally severed the phone and cable-TV lines to our house. He took me outside and showed me the two wires dangling from the pole.

I was bummed, but at that point not angry. I told Wilfredo not to worry, then got on my mobile phone and called our phone company, AT&T. The person I spoke to immediately grasped the problem—namely, the telephone wire was cut—and said he would send a repair truck right away, which he did. The phone line was fixed in about an hour.

After speaking to AT&T I called the cable-TV company, which I will call "Bomcast," although that is not its real name. Its real name is Comcast.

After waiting on hold for a while and then going through a menu, I was able to speak to a Bomcast customer service representative in a distant land where English is not the first or even necessarily the second language. I did not record our conversation, but this is basically how it went (and if you think I am exaggerating, you have never been serviced by Bomcast):

REPRESENTATIVE: May I have your name so that I can gratuitously repeat it?

ME: David Barry.

REPRESENTATIVE: Thank you, David. How may I help you today, David?

ME: Our cable TV is out. The yard guy accidentally cut the cable.

REPRESENTATIVE: David, I understand you are saying that your cable television is not working.

ME: Right. The yard guy cut the cable.

REPRESENTATIVE: David, I am sorry that your cable television is not working. I will get this problem resolved for you, David.

ME: Thank you.

REPRESENTATIVE: David, can you tell me how many cable boxes you have in your house?

ME: Four.

REPRESENTATIVE: Thank you, David. And can you tell me, David, if the cable is working in any of those TVs, David?

ME: No. It's not working anywhere. There's no cable TV coming into the house. The cable was cut. With hedge trimmers. I can see the wire dangling from the pole.

REPRESENTATIVE: Thank you, David. So I understand you are saying that none of your cable boxes are working at this time.

ME: Right, we don't have cable service, but it's got nothing to do with the boxes. The problem is that our cable was physically cut. The cable wire is not physically connected to the house. So somebody needs to come and fix the wire.

REPRESENTATIVE: Thank you, David, I will resolve this issue for you, David.

ME: Great, thanks.

(There is a lengthy pause here during which I start to worry that we have become disconnected. Finally the representative gets back on the line.)

REPRESENTATIVE: Can you please do me a favor, David?

ME: Sure.

REPRESENTATIVE: David, I want you to please go to your main cable box and unplug the power cord. Then wait thirty seconds and plug it back in. Can you do that for me, David?

ME: Why?

REPRESENTATIVE: This will reset your cable box, David.

ME: But the problem *isn't the cable box*. The problem is that *the cable wire was cut*.

REPRESENTATIVE: David, we can sometimes restore the cable service by resetting the cable box, David. David David David.

ME: Please listen to me. The problem is *not the cable box*. The problem is that *the cable wire was cut*. Do you understand? The cable wire is now in two separate pieces that are not connected to each other, so the television programs can't get into the house. You need to SEND SOMEBODY TO FIX THE WIRE, OK?

(There is another pause.)

REPRESENTATIVE: David, can you please tell me the model number of your main cable box?

I admit that at that point I lost my temper and yelled at the representative. I imagine that when he went home that night, he said to his significant other, in his native language, something like: "You would not *believe* the moron I got stuck with servicing today! He couldn't even understand how to unplug his cable box!"

Eventually I was able to talk to a different Bomcast person, who agreed, somewhat reluctantly, that the problem was probably that the cable had been severed, and scheduled a service appointment. Afterward I felt bad about getting so angry at the first person I spoke to. It really wasn't his fault. It was the fault of the Bomcast executives who decided that their customer service would be provided by people in distant lands whose training consists of being handed a script that appears to be based on an Abbott and Costello routine.

I have a fantasy. In this fantasy, late one night a cable executive calls 911, only to discover that, as a cost-cutting measure, the police department has outsourced its 911 operation to the cable company:

OPERATOR: Thank you for choosing 911. What is your emergency?

EXECUTIVE: A man broke into my house! He has an ax!

OPERATOR: May I have your name and address?

EXECUTIVE: Bob Timmons, 123 Belchwater Road. Please hurry!

OPERATOR: Thank you, Bob. Bob, I understand you are saying you have an intruder in your house?

EXECUTIVE: Yes! With an ax! Please send somebody!

OPERATOR: Bob, I am sorry that an intruder with an ax is in your house, and I will help you to resolve this problem.

EXECUTIVE: Please hurry! He's coming up the stairs!

OPERATOR: Bob, in order to assist you, I am going to need to ask you some questions. Is that OK, Bob?

EXECUTIVE: Yes! Just hurry!

OPERATOR: Bob, first, can you tell me, did you give permission for this intruder to enter your house, Bob?

EXECUTIVE: No, for God's sake! He broke in! With an ax!

OPERATOR: Thank you, Bob. I understand you are saying that the intruder does not have your permission to be in your house at 123 Elkwater Road, is that correct?

EXECUTIVE: No! I'm at 123 *Belchwater* Road!

OPERATOR: So, Bob, you're saying you are at 123 Belchwater Road?

EXECUTIVE: Yes!

OPERATOR: But the intruder is at 123 *Elkwater* Road, Bob?

EXECUTIVE: NO! HE'S HERE! HE'S BREAKING DOWN THE
BEDROOM DOOR! FOR THE LOVE OF GOD SEND HELP!!

OPERATOR: Bob, so that I can better assist you, can you
please describe the ax?

*(On the executive's end of the line, there are shouts, sounds
of a struggle, screams, then silence. A new voice comes on
the line.)*

VOICE: Who is this?

OPERATOR: This is 911. Is this Bob?

VOICE: No.

OPERATOR: Do you have an emergency?

VOICE: Not anymore.

OPERATOR: So the problem has been resolved?

VOICE: Yes.

OPERATOR: Would you be willing to take a brief customer-
satisfaction survey regarding your 911 experience?

VOICE: Sure.

At this point you're thinking, *Dave, isn't it a bit extreme
to fantasize about a cable-TV executive being chopped to*

death with an ax? Wouldn't life in prison be punishment enough?

Of course you're right, assuming you mean in solitary confinement. But my point is, I have anger issues. I get disproportionately annoyed by behaviors that people engage in all the time. So I am angry a lot, and I usually hold my anger in. I bathe in bile. I let it fester and churn inside me, which can't be healthy. On the other hand, if I let my anger out, people would think I was insane, and they would be correct, because I'd be out in public shouting things like "YOU ALREADY SAMPLED THE CO-CONUT BOYSENBERRY RUTABAGA KALE SWIRL! NOW MAKE UP YOUR GODDAMN MIND!!"

So what's the answer?

The answer, which will probably not surprise you, is to learn a Lesson from Lucy.

Does Lucy get angry? Of course she does. As I have mentioned, she becomes irate when men come and take away our hard-earned garbage. And sometimes, when we're outside looking for exactly the right place to make a crucial weewee, we will encounter a dog that Lucy decides—for some subtle dog reason that I am incapable of sensing, although I would not question Lucy's judgment—is an asshole.

Lucy also hates the Goodyear blimp, which occasionally flies over our house. Apparently back in prehistoric times a primitive blimp did something horrible to Lucy's ancestors, and she has not forgotten or forgiven. When the Goodyear blimp appears, she barks furiously at it until it goes away, which it always does, because, for all its size and fame, it is a coward.

So Lucy definitely gets angry. But not often, and—this is the important thing—never for long. The instant the cause of her anger is gone, she's over it, a calm and carefree dog once again, snoozing and farting. She does not dwell on past irritations. She lets her anger go.

I need to learn to do that. I'm not saying that I can, or even should, completely ignore the world's jerks. But I need to accept certain realities:

- My hating a jerk for jerky behavior doesn't hurt the jerk at all. The jerk, being a jerk, is unaware of my feelings. So all I'm doing, by marinating in my anger, is making myself unhappy.
- Most of the time, the annoyance caused by jerk behavior is minor and short-lived. We're talking about waiting a few seconds longer in line, that kind of thing. It's rarely worth stressing about, or creating a confrontation over.

- If I got to know the strangers who annoy me, I'd probably discover that some of them—maybe most of them—really aren't such bad people. I might even like them.
- Except the guy revving the Harley. He is vermin.

No, seriously, even the Harley guy probably has redeeming qualities. Most people do, if you give them a chance. And if they don't—if they're really just awful people—then their lives are already miserable. My hatred won't make them feel any worse. It's a waste of my time; it saps my energy and sours my life.

So here's the fourth Lesson from Lucy:

Let Go of Your Anger,
Unless It's About Something Really Important,
Which It Almost Never Is.

I definitely need to learn this lesson. I need to relax, to chill, to forgive and forget (or at least to forget). I need to inhale deeply and exhale slowly, to let all that rage and stress and tension flow out of me like some kind of (I apologize for this image) emotional enema.

You know who else needs to learn this lesson?

Everybody.

I'm serious. The whole world is *way* too angry these days. If you want proof of that, don some eye protection and take a look at Facebook.

In case you just woke up from a coma, I should explain that Facebook is a social-media website that literally billions of people visit regularly for the purpose of making some person named Mark Zuckerberg insanely rich. When you join Facebook, you get your own virtual "page," on which you can post text, photos, videos, links to articles, etc. Then you become "friends" with other Facebook users; you and your friends can see and interact with each other's pages.

I joined Facebook because I have a lot of relatives and friends on there, and it's a good way to maintain human relationships without having to see or talk to other humans. You can read about people's life milestones, such as birthdays, weddings, anniversaries and deaths. You can see pictures of their kids, grandkids, vacations, pets, wounds,[20] etc. You also see a lot of pictures of food, because some people apparently view everything they eat as a life milestone.

---

20 Seriously: I have seen people's wounds on Facebook.

My favorite thing about Facebook is that you can express your reactions to people's life events simply by clicking on emojis, which are little face drawings depicting emotions. As I write this, the available emojis are "Like," "Love," "Haha," "Wow," "Sad" and "Angry." So if one of your Facebook friends has a death in the family, instead of taking on the tedious chore of writing a letter or calling, you can simply click on "Sad," and just like that, bada-bing bada-boom, you have registered your sincere emotional reaction, and you can get on with your busy life.

OK, so it's kind of perfunctory. But it's better than nothing, and it has enabled me, a pathologically detached person (see the first Lesson from Lucy), to stay at least loosely in touch with people I care about. That's why I go on Facebook. I like the social aspect.

What I dislike is the political aspect, which infests Facebook like a toxic mold. I don't go to Facebook for politics. I'd rather see wounds.

I'm not saying people don't have a right to express their political views. Obviously they have the right to say whatever they want, and the right to not care what I think about it. I just wish people wouldn't use Facebook for politics. I get politics spewed at me almost everywhere else

I go on the Internet. I'd rather not also see it sandwiched between pictures of people's grandkids.

It's not the specific political views I dislike; it's the tone. I wouldn't mind if people said something like, "Hey, here's what I think about this issue, and here's why." And maybe even: "What do *you* think? Let's have an open-minded discussion!"

But that's almost never the tone. The default tone of political discourse—and not just on Facebook; it's everywhere—is angry, even CAPS LOCK ANGRY. It is also often wildly melodramatic. Everything that happens is THE WORST THING THAT EVER HAPPENED. And to round out the unpleasantness, the tone is also often lecture-y, sneering, contemptuous, condescending, self-righteous, smug. No matter what the issue is, the message is: *This is what I think, and there can be NO DISCUSSION about it because the only possible reason you could have a different opinion is that you are stupid, or evil, or stupid AND evil.*

Perhaps you're a conservative, and you think I'm talking about progressives here.

Or perhaps you're a progressive, and you think I'm talking about conservatives.

Either way, you're wrong. I'm talking about *you*.

I'm not saying don't care about politics.

I'm not saying don't stand up for what you believe in.

I'm not saying don't debate people you disagree with.

What I'm saying is: Don't hate them. Try talking to them, instead of calling them names. Try *listening* to them. And even if you disagree with them—even if you *hate* what they're saying—don't let your hate consume you. Remain calm. Inhale. Exhale. Remember this: however bad you think things are today, however awful you consider our leaders to be, however stupid you think your fellow Americans are, this country has seen worse times, including—to name a few—the Civil War, 9/11, the Great Depression and six seasons of *Jersey Shore*. We muddled through those times. We will muddle through these.

So let go of your anger. Even if you think I'm a naïve fool to be optimistic about the future, you should *still* let go of your anger. It's not helping your cause, and it's not hurting the people you perceive as your enemies. Mainly what it's doing is making you unhappy.

Just let it go.

And, Comcast, if you're reading this: I forgive you.

For now.

THE FIFTH LESSON FROM LUCY

Sometimes when we're walking Lucy we encounter a male neighborhood dog whom I will call Brutus, in case he reads this. I don't know what specific breed of dog Brutus is, so I will describe him to you: Brutus is ugly. He looks like a cross between a dog and a toad. He's short and squat, with a very flat face such as a breed might develop after many generations of repeatedly running face-first at high speed into sliding glass doors. Brutus's eyes are far apart and bulbous; they protrude so far that you fear they're going to pop out and roll off down the sidewalk. To complete his look, Brutus has a pronounced underbite, with teeth jutting randomly from the bottom of his drooling mouth.

So Brutus is not what you would call a visual treat.

But do not try to tell him that. Brutus believes himself to be a stud muffin. When he sees Lucy, he lunges boldly toward her, dragging his owner by the leash. Panting excitedly, Brutus bounces around Lucy on his stumpy legs, doing leash-tangling laps, looking for an angle that will enable him to attain some level of intimacy, which because of the height differential would be impossible without some kind of ramp. Still, Brutus persists, thrusting his flat snout up as close to her butt region as he is able to get, making it clear with every quivering inch of his small mutant canine body that he is *ready to party*.

As for Lucy: she is interested. She wags her tail; she takes deep appreciative whiffs of Brutus as he orbits her. This is as far as things ever get, because after a minute or two we owners separate the dogs so we can continue our walks. But for a little while there, magic is happening. Love is in the air. Where I see a genetic mistake, Lucy sees a beautiful being.

This is often the case when dogs meet. Granted, sometimes two dogs will take an instant dislike to each other, and some dogs, especially your yappy hand-carried microdogs, seem to hate pretty much everybody, dog or human. But for the most part, in my experience, a dog, when it meets another dog, will respond as follows:

HEY! YOU'RE A DOG AND I'M A DOG! HOLY SMOKES, WE'RE BOTH DOGS!!! LET'S SMELL EACH OTHER'S PERSONAL REGIONS! WOW! YOU ARE GIVING OFF A STRONG DOG AROMA THAT I FIND INTRIGUING! LET'S SMELL EACH OTHER'S REGIONS SOME MORE! WOW! LET'S SMELL EACH OTHER'S REGIONS SOME MORE! WOW! LET'S SMELL EACH OTHER'S REGIONS SOME . . .

And so on. The dogs will enthusiastically explore each other, and then they will play with each other. If the circumstances are right, they might even commence humping operations. They will do these things regardless of what breed of dog each dog is, or what size it is, or how old it is, or what it looks like. For the purpose of humping operations, some male dogs don't even care if the other dog is actually a *dog*. A human leg, or an ottoman, or (I have seen this with my own eyes) a chain saw that happens to be lying on the ground—these can all serve as desirable sex partners for a motivated guy dog.

This is a beautiful thing about dogs. Not that they will hump a power tool—although you have to admire that "can-do" spirit—but that they do not judge by appearance. They don't care what they look like—they don't even *know* what they look like—and they don't care what anybody else looks like. I won't go so far as to say that they judge others purely by their inner spiritual qualities. But they clearly are not hung up on looks.

Whereas of course we humans are *obsessed* with looks. We mess constantly with the appearance of our faces, our hair, our bodies. We starve ourselves. We have surgery on our breasts, noses, chins, cheeks, eyelids, ears, necks, arms, stomachs and butts in an effort to make them look more like somebody else's breasts, noses, chins, etc. We pay people to inject Botox into our faces. We pay people to stick tubes into our thighs and suck out the fat. *We pay people to put strips of hot wax on our genitals and then rip them off.* (I mean they rip off the strips; the genitals usually remain attached.)

No dog would ever do any of these things. If a dog were capable of (a) speech, and (b) grasping the concept of genital waxing, that dog would say: "I may drink from the toilet, but I would never do THAT."

Why are we humans so obsessed with appearance? The unfortunate truth is, it's hardwired into human biology. Modern humans evolved around a hundred thousand years ago during the Pleistocene Epoch, which gets its name from the fact that in those days there was a lot of pleistocene around. In order for their species to survive, these early humans had to reproduce by—follow me closely—having sex with each other. The humans who were better at reproducing produced more offspring, which means they were more likely to pass their genes along to future generations than the humans who were not so good at reproducing. This is how evolution works.

So let's consider two Pleistocene males, Bob and Fred (not their real names). Bob is thoughtful, quiet and shy. Physically, he's on the small side and not aggressive. He enjoys admiring the beauty of a sunset and taking long, quiet walks on the beach, assuming they had beaches in that epoch. Bob has sexual urges, but he wants the sex to be part of a multifaceted and mutually rewarding relationship, not just a physical act. When he meets a female he is attracted to—we'll call her Naomi—he takes it slow, because he wants to get to know her and give her time to get to know him. He wants to make sure they are truly *right* for each other.

Fred is larger and more muscular than Bob, and much more aggressive. He attempts to mate with pretty much every female he encounters. If a female lets him know that she is not interested via some body-language indicator such as hitting Fred in the face with a rock, Fred is undeterred; he simply moves on to the next female, confident that sooner or later he will score.

And score he does. Certain Pleistocene females—we will call them Mabels—prefer a large, aggressive male, because they believe he will be better able to protect them and hunt for them and bring home a nice haunch of mastodon for dinner. Over the course of his lifetime, Fred will copulate with dozens of females, including Naomi, who has grown tired of waiting for Bob to get up enough courage to ask her to the Pleistocene Prom.

So ask yourself: Which of these males is going to pass along more of his genes to succeeding generations?

That's right: the late Hugh Hefner.

I am kidding, of course. Hugh did not evolve until the early Holocene Epoch. Obviously Fred was the winner in the Reproduction Derby. Succeeding generations of humans contained more Freds and Mabels than Bobs and whomever Bob managed to attract.

This selection process continued for many thousands of years. Eventually, as civilization got more civilized, physical traits became less crucial for human survival. Today a woman does not need a man to provide her with a mastodon haunch; she can order one from Amazon.[21] But after eons of dominance by the Fred/Mabel genes,

---

21   For all I know this is actually true.

modern humans still have a tendency to be attracted toward a certain kind of look. Researchers have done studies wherein they display photos of a variety of people and ask subjects to judge them on attractiveness. The results of these studies are summarized by Wikipedia as follows:

> *Men, on average, tend to be attracted to women who are shorter than they are, have a youthful appearance, and exhibit features such as a symmetrical face, full breasts, full lips, and a low waist-hip ratio. Women, on average, tend to be attracted to men who are taller than they are, display a high degree of facial symmetry, masculine facial dimorphism, and who have broad shoulders, a relatively narrow waist, and a V-shaped torso.*

If that sounds too technical, and you don't feel like looking up "dimorphism," let me translate it into layperson's terms: scientific tests show that, in general, people are attracted to people who probably don't look like you.

OK, maybe I'm projecting a little here. Maybe you actually do have the preferred physical characteristics. Maybe you look like Brad Pitt or Beyoncé or Channing Tatum or Scarlett Johansson or Denzel Washington or Penélope Cruz or the late Bruce Lee or additional examples of attractive people from every major racial and ethnic group because I do not wish to get into trouble here. If so, good for you.

But many people do not have the look that the Fred/ Mabel genes find attractive. Me, for example. I don't look like the kind of man who, in primitive times, would have participated in the mastodon hunt. I look like the kind of man who would have remained a safe distance away, making comical wisecracks about the mastodon hunters ("Expose your armpits, Fred! That should bring it down!"). I wouldn't make these wisecracks loud enough that the hunters could actually *hear* me; my strategy would be to use humor to impress primitive females, so they would want to mate with me. But of course that wouldn't work: they were primitive but not stupid. They didn't need jokes. They needed protein.

Granted that was long ago. In modern times, many women, when surveyed, say that one of the qualities they find most attractive in a man is a sense of humor. They *say* this, and I think they really believe it. They want to see themselves as the kind of person who is attracted to a sense of humor.

But their *genes* still want Fred.

I base this broad[22] generalization on my extensive experience as a class clown attempting to attract females with my zany wit, only to fail miserably time after time. This pattern began when, after an innocent, carefree boyhood spent blowing up mailboxes, I lurched awkwardly into adolescence. I still have memories—*vivid* memories—of that hellish time. It was like one of those horror movies wherein alien beings take over people's bodies one by one, except that instead of alien beings, it was puberty. One day, the girl who sat next to you in class would be a girl. The next day, you'd look over and there would be this *woman*. With *bosoms*. The boys were also undergoing major bodily renovations, although generally not as early; I personally did not achieve full puberty until roughly age thirty-seven.

But if my physical change was annoyingly slow, my emotional change was abrupt. Suddenly, all of these vague feelings and yearnings I'd had throughout childhood had a specific, urgent focus. (*Bosoms!*) I became very, very interested in sex, and how it worked, and above all whether there was any conceivable scenario wherein

---

22 Har har.

I personally would be able to engage in it. Fortunately, back then boys my age had access to a vast storehouse of solid information on this topic in the form of slightly older boys, who—although they had no direct personal experience with sex, either—had heard various reliable rumors from boys slightly older than they were, who had acquired this information from slightly older boys, who allegedly knew somebody slightly older who claimed to have actually engaged in some activity that could be construed as sex.

To augment this knowledge base, boys back then had another major information resource on human sexuality in the form of the massive national strategic stockpile of old *Playboy* magazines stored under the mattresses of the nation's older brothers. In terms of commitment to recycling, the "green" movement of today has nothing on the older brothers of the fifties and sixties, who never threw away a *Playboy* and who risked a lifetime of back ailments by courageously sleeping on mattresses distorted by magazine mounds the size of a dead horse.

I didn't have an older brother, but I had friends who did, and we spent many hours enhancing our understanding of human sexuality by staring at heavily airbrushed photographs of naked women with breasts like weather balloons. We were aflame with adolescent hormonal urges, and highly prone to spontaneous boners, which could strike anywhere, anytime, even in the teeming halls of Harold C. Crittenden Junior High School, where you had to be ready at a moment's notice to hold your Earth science textbook in an unnatural frontal position to hide the tent pole in your khakis.

So my innocent boyhood was over. Now I was interested—*really* interested—in girls, especially cute ones. The problem was, cute girls were not interested in me, at least not as boyfriend material. They were interested in the cute guys, the cool guys, the athletes, the studs, none of which I was. I was the small funny kid with glasses. At parties, I could get the cute girls to laugh, but when it was time to play Seven Minutes in Heaven, they always wound up going into the closet with cute guys. I never had any minutes in heaven. I didn't have a *nanosecond* in heaven.

I came to hate the way I looked. Before puberty, I paid basically zero attention to my appearance. But I spent the vast majority of seventh, eighth and ninth grades staring at the bathroom mirror through my thick Macy's Optical Department lenses, wishing that somebody different were staring back. I wanted desperately to be bigger, handsomer, studlier, more like the guys who the cute girls were interested in.

You're probably thinking: *How very sad for you, Dave, but did you ever stop wallowing in self-pity long enough to realize that there were nice, smart, funny girls at Harold C. Crittenden Junior High who, like you, didn't happen to inherit the preferred-appearance genes? Did it ever occur to you to be interested in* them?

Of course not! I was a self-absorbed adolescent nitwit. I hereby apologize to the girls of Harold C. whom I never wanted to go into the closet with, not that you necessarily would have wanted to go in there with me.

Eventually I got older and, if not wiser, at least less stupid. My self-esteem improved, and I got better at appreciating qualities in other people beyond simply how they look. Also I got contact lenses.

But I still have emotional scars from those hideous adolescent years. I remain, after all this time, fundamentally insecure about my appearance. I'm still intimidated by really good-looking people. Intellectually, I know the whole concept of "good-looking" is, in modern times, arbitrary and unfair. I know it's ridiculous that millions of people are obsessed to the point of worship with, for example, Kim Kardashian, who has the genetically de-

sirable waist-to-hip ratio but also the IQ of a lawn orna-
ment. I know that the attributes we should value most
in other people are nonphysical: intelligence, sense of
humor, honesty, wisdom, sense of humor, courage, gen-
erosity, sense of humor and of course sense of humor.

I know these things, intellectually.

And yet, when I see an attractive woman—defined as
"a woman who is by no means as attractive as my wife"—
some primitive Fred part of my brain goes, quote, *whoa.*
If I am being totally honest, I will admit that I'm more interested in talking to that woman than to a woman who
does not elicit the *whoa.* I'm not proud of this; I am in
fact ashamed of it. But I can't deny it.

And I don't think I'm exceptional. I think most of us
humans have trouble disregarding physical appearance.
Whatever genetic tendencies we have are constantly re-
inforced by a culture that is utterly obsessed with beauty,
a culture that bombards us relentlessly in every medium
with images of the preferred physical template. One
glance at almost any movie or TV show and we know
who the heroes are: the hot people.

Here's an example that I find particularly annoying:
Beauty and the Beast. In theory, this story preaches the
right message: looks don't matter; *character* matters. The

heroine, Belle, who is of course beautiful, overcomes her revulsion at the Beast's hideous appearance and learns to love him for his inner self. Which sounds fine, except that in the end, the Beast *turns back into a handsome prince.* It's a Happy Ending! Featuring an ideal level of facial dimorphism!

In other words, the message was complete bullshit. If it had been serious, the Beast would have stayed a beast, and he and Belle would have produced unusual-looking hybrid offspring who, when they reached adolescence, would have returned to the castle sobbing after parties because they weren't chosen for Seven Minutes in Heaven.

I have the same problem with the fairy tale of the Ugly Duckling, whose life sucks because he is ugly, but then, in the Happy Ending, he transforms into a beautiful swan. Yay for him, but what about all the ugly ducklings that transform into ugly ducks?

Of course real ducks, as opposed to fairy-tale ducks, probably don't care that much about physical appearance. Animals generally don't seem to be nearly as picky about looks as we are. They're more like, "Hey, we both belong to the same species; that's good enough for me."

Which brings us back to Lucy and her admirer, Brutus.

Or Lucy and pretty much any other dog—or, for that matter, any human. Lucy doesn't judge you by what you look like. And in that regard, she's a better person than I am.

So here's the Lucy lesson of this chapter:

Try Not to Judge People by Their Looks,
and Don't Obsess Over Your Own.

I say "try" because I think this is a difficult lesson to put into practice, as it goes against our biological programming. Also, there are times when it's OK to judge by appearance; if you meet a man with a swastika tattooed on his forehead, you don't need to seek out his sensitive side.

But most of the time looks don't tell a person's story. Life has taught me that there are plenty of beautiful people who are shallow and boring, and there are plenty of nonbeautiful people who are deep and fascinating and fun. Which of course means they're the truly beautiful ones. The trick to finding them is to be looking with more than just your eyes.

As I say, I've gotten better about this over the years. And I spend a lot less time than I used to fretting about my own appearance. One of the positive aspects of aging is that, as you and your friends get old, you pretty much give up on being hot; you're happy just being not dead yet.

Still, it's a struggle. Fred and Mabel still lurk in my genes; it's going to take a conscious effort to overcome them.

But I'm trying. I'm trying to look at everyone differently. And when I say "everyone," I mean to include Brutus. Lucy's absolutely right: He's a beautiful dog. They're *all* beautiful dogs.

THE SIXTH LESSON FROM LUCY

While I was writing this book, Florida got nailed by Hurricane Irma. I want to state right up front that my family and I came through it OK. I'm not seeking pity, and I don't want you to think I'm a sniveling whiner. (I *am* a sniveling whiner; I just don't want you to think so.)

I know that the hurricane season was unimaginably worse for people in other areas, especially Puerto Rico. I also know that other parts of the world have their own kinds of natural disasters—earthquakes, tornadoes, floods, the New Jersey Turnpike—which can be just as bad as hurricanes, or worse.

But a hurricane is a special kind of torture. A lot of it is mental torture, but it can be excruciating. And the anxiety never goes completely away, because when a hurricane season ends, you know that another one is coming, and that eventually, if you stay in Florida long enough, you WILL get nailed.

"So why do you stay there?" non-Floridians often ask.

For one thing, we usually don't get nailed. We can go years between nailings. And during those years there will be many winter mornings when we turn on the TV news at breakfast and see a headline like BLIZZARD BLASTS NORTHEAST, with video of cars skidding off icy roads and wretched parka-clad people staggering through waist-high snowdrifts pursued by wolves. In *Times Square*.

We Floridians see this, and then—as we look outside and see the sun shining down from a bright-blue sky on palm trees swaying in the gentle tropical breeze—we cannot help but smile and take a celebratory sip from our margarita. Yes, we're having a margarita for breakfast; that's how happy we are not to be up north. We wonder why you Northerners stay up *there*, where there's no un-certainty about the misery of winter: you're going to get it every year, for months at a time, forever. We'll take the occasional hurricane over that anytime.

Anytime, that is, except when an actual hurricane is heading our way. Then we start to get nervous. Then we panic. Then we go insane.

I blame the TV news people. Oh, they mean well. They want to inform us and keep us safe. They want to Serve the Community! But what they always do, in the end, is drive the community batshit crazy.

It starts with the Perky TV Weatherperson. In South Florida this is usually an attractive young woman wearing an extremely form-fitting cocktail dress and approximately forty-five pounds of eyeliner. On most days the Perky Weatherperson's job is to tell us, via a visual-extravaganza presentation lasting upwards of five minutes and involving a vast array of technology including radar and satellite imagery, dazzling graphics, a green screen and many, many statistics, that it is going to be warm and humid with a chance of thunderstorms. We already know this, of course; Florida has been warm and humid with a chance of thunderstorms basically every day for several million years. If the TV station wanted to cut costs, it could simply record a Perky Weatherperson forecast and replay it forever, using computerized effects to vary the color of her cocktail dress.

So most of the time we Floridians are paying more attention to the weather forecaster than to her forecast. But our attitude changes radically when a hurricane is coming.

It starts when the hurricane is maybe ten days away. We notice that the Perky Weatherperson, all of a sudden, has a frowny face. She's showing us a map of the Caribbean with a little hurricane symbol and a cone showing its expected path. The cone is pointing roughly in our direction.

Now the Perky Weatherperson has our attention. She shows us computer models, with lines indicating where various computers (some of which have apparently been smoking crack) predict the hurricane will ultimately go. The lines swarm all over the map; some head toward Mexico, some toward the US mainland, some toward Bermuda, with maybe one or two making direct hits on Iceland. Basically the computers think the hurricane could go anywhere. Including Florida.

"We'll be keeping an eye on this," says the Perky Weatherperson.

At this point we're starting to feel nervous, but we're not yet panicking. We're assuming that the hurricane will go somewhere else. In fact, we are fervently hoping for this. This is one of the ugly truths about hurricanes: you root for them to hit other people. You don't *admit* this, of course. But if a hurricane is getting close, and it looks like it's going to either hit Miami or veer north and nail Palm

Beach, I guarantee you that everybody in each of these cities is praying that it will whack the other one.

Over the next few days everybody gets more nervous as the hurricane creeps closer and the Perky Weatherperson gets frownier. Now the other TV news people are getting involved, offering helpful hurricane-preparedness tips such as:

- Make sure you have enough food, water and batteries to last for a week after the hurricane passes.
- Fill your car with gas and get some cash.
- Remove yard debris and get ready to put up your hurricane shutters.
- You are GOING TO DIE.

They don't say that last tip out loud, but you can see it in their frowns.

Now the hurricane map is on the TV all the time. The cone is getting closer, and the computer models, even the ones on crack, are starting to agree that Florida is a likely target. This is when we Floridians go from nervousness to panic. We rush to our local Publix supermarket, which is mobbed with other panicking Floridians, and we buy as many items as we can cram into our shopping cart, and then we fill another cart. We buy enough bottled water to fill an Olympic pool. We buy whatever batteries have not already been grabbed. We have been known to buy nine-volt batteries even though we have nothing at home that uses nine-volt batteries, because the TV people keep telling us *we need to have batteries.*

All of us buy bleach. We don't know why. I believe that many years ago a shrewd thinker in the Clorox marketing department came up with the idea of starting the rumor that it was vital to have bleach in a hurricane. So now it's a tradition among panicked Floridians to grab a large bottle of Clorox and lug it home, even though (a) we already have at least one large bottle of Clorox at home, and (b) we have no earthly idea what purpose bleach is supposed to serve in a hurricane. We put the new Clorox bottle on the shelf next to our previous Clorox bottles and our nine-volt batteries. Preparedness!

Mainly we buy food. We buy tuna and Spam and sandwich makings and canned soup and many snacks in the form of candy and chips and enough granola bars and peanut-butter crackers to supply a cruise ship for six months at sea. We buy food that we would never buy if our brains were functioning properly. For example, as Irma is approaching, Michelle buys lentils. We never eat lentils; she has never cooked lentils. I am not totally certain what lentils are. They look like a bag of gravel. I ask Michelle why she bought lentils, and she tells me it's because they don't spoil. I am tempted to note that the same could also be said of, for example, linoleum. But I do not, because Michelle would not see the humor. She has gone insane. We have all gone insane.

At this point the hurricane is still three days away, but it's all anybody can think about. We are definitely in the cone. The cone is everywhere on TV, including Depends commercials. The TV news people are frowning so hard that their forehead makeup sometimes bursts into flames.

We spend a day putting up shutters and bringing in loose objects from our yard, because we have been told countless times by the frowning TV people that during the storm these could become Deadly Missiles. We bring *everything* inside. We bring in filthy insect-infested potted plants that have been festering and rotting in the subtropical swelter of our yard for years. They are disgusting, but we welcome them into our home because otherwise we fear that they will become airborne Planters of Doom, hurtling through the neighborhood and crashing through somebody's wall in a deadly hail of ceramic shards and irate millipedes.

You think that's crazy, right? I agree! It's crazy! That's my point. *We have gone completely insane.*

Now the hurricane is two days away. On the TV news they're showing us video of desperate people lining up at Home Depot to buy plywood. We wonder: *Should we go to Home Depot and line up to buy plywood?* We already have window protection, so we don't know what we would DO with the plywood, any more than we know what to do with the bleach. But still the worrying thought nags at us: The hurricane is coming and *we have no plywood.* WE HAVE NO PLYWOOD!

Now the hurricane is one day away. We are done preparing; we have nothing to do and nowhere to go. Schools, businesses, stores and restaurants are all closed. We are nervous and bored at the same time. We feel helpless, just sitting around. We want to take *action.*

And so we do. Specifically, we eat. It is a statistical fact that the average Florida household consumes 93 percent of its emergency post-hurricane food reserves before the hurricane actually arrives. I think this might be a primitive survival instinct: our bodies want to become much heavier, so that the hurricane winds will be unable to pick us up and turn us into Deadly Missiles. Whatever the cause, we spend the last pre-hurricane day eating our food supply, starting with the most desirable items and munching our way down the hierarchy, as follows:

1. Candy
2. Cookies
3. Chips
4. Sandwiches
5. Tuna
6. Soup
7. Spam
8. Potted plants
9. Cannibalism
10. Lentils

Now the hurricane is only hours away. The TV news people are receiving on-air forehead Botox transfusions from fifty-five-gallon drums. Every few minutes they cut away to one of their excited reporters standing on a beach, wearing a rain slicker with the station logo on it. The excited reporters always make two observations:

1. The wind is starting to pick up!
2. Everybody should stay away from this beach that I am standing on!

These observations are, even by TV news standards, remarkably idiotic. But they are part of the traditional Kabuki theater of hurricane coverage in the hours just before the storm. We Floridians find them almost comforting as we stare at the TV screen and chew, cowlike, on our post-hurricane food reserves.

Night falls. Outside it's getting windy and rainy, but the brunt of the storm is still not here. To pass the time, we decide to watch a DVD of the 1958 film *South Pacific*, which tells the story of a group of plucky World War II American naval personnel on a South Pacific island who thwart the invading Japanese troops by staging elaborate musical numbers.

JAPANESE SCOUT *(peering at the American base through binoculars)*: I don't like this one bit.

SECOND JAPANESE SCOUT: What is it?

FIRST SCOUT: Take a look!

SECOND SCOUT *(peering through binoculars)*: It's an American sailor . . . He's wearing a grass skirt and . . . is that a *coconut-shell brassiere*?

FIRST SCOUT: They're up to something! We need to tell headquarters!

SECOND SCOUT: Wait, how come we're speaking English?

South Pacific is a fine musical, and it helps us take our minds off Irma for a couple of hours. We hum along with the show tunes, munching our post-hurricane food reserves in a more relaxed manner.

Then the DVD ends.

Then Irma arrives.

She blows hard all night long. She blows like a banshee for twelve solid hours. As a professional writer, I am required by union rules to describe the hurricane as sounding like a freight train. And it does, sort of. But Irma sounds more like a huge, clumsy ghost, moaning and howling and making loud thumping and crashing sounds in the dark. What is truly weird is that, over the howl of the hurricane, we can hear a very loud chorus of . . . frogs. Ordinarily we never hear frogs, but during the hurricane, with monsoon rains fire-hosing against our windows and wind gusts approaching one hundred miles an hour, the frogs are croaking their lungs out, as if to say, "THIS IS *OUR TIME, BABY*! WE'RE PARTYING AMPHIBIAN STYLE! WE'RE POOPING ON YOUR PATIO! WE'RE LICKING THE STEAK JUICE OFF YOUR BARBECUE GRILL WITH OUR ICKY FROG TONGUES, AND THERE IS *NOTHING YOU CAN DO ABOUT IT*!!"

It's a long, long night. Our electricity keeps flickering,

going out, coming back. Finally around five a.m. we lose it altogether. Fortunately, we have a large propane generator that can power the whole house. It fires up, and our lights and air-conditioning come back on. Unfortunately, our phone, Internet and cable TV are all out, and our cell service is almost nonexistent. Tragically, our digital bathroom scale is still working.

But we're OK. Heavier, but OK.

Daylight finally arrives; after a couple of hours the wind starts to abate. We go outside to survey the damage. Many trees and power lines are down, along with roughly a billion leaves and branches, covering the lawns and sidewalks, blocking the streets with a tangled jumble of green. But our house is OK, as are most of the houses in the neighborhood. Other areas, such as the Florida Keys, took far worse hits. As we encounter neighbors emerging from their homes, we all say the same thing: "We were lucky."

And we *are* lucky, no question about it. But we have not yet escaped the misery that hurricanes inflict. We have simply entered a new phase, which, mental-torture-wise, may be the worst: waiting. We're waiting for the roads to be cleared, waiting for businesses and schools to reopen, waiting for life to feel at least somewhat normal again.

Above all we're waiting for the electricity to come back. If you've ever gone for more than a few hours without electricity/Internet/phone/cable, you know how quickly it becomes an all-consuming obsession: *When will it come back?*

At the risk of sounding blasphemous, I would compare power restoration to the Rapture, which, some Christians believe, is an unknown time in the future when God will snatch the righteous off the face of the Earth and take them up to heaven. Getting your power back is like that, except instead of God deciding who gets raptured, it's Florida Power & Light.

But the process is equally mysterious. Suddenly the houses across the street from you will get power, or even—this is almost unbearably cruel—the house *right next door* will get power, and your house will remain dark. Sometimes your neighbors will have power for *days*, and you still won't. Sometimes you'll get power for an hour or two, and just when you're starting to relax, *it goes away again.* After a few days of this you become desperate. You start to wonder if the electricity god has forgotten you, or if you have done something to offend it. (*Maybe I should have bought plywood.*) You would sacrifice a goat if you thought it would bring your power back, and you had a goat.

Fortunately, as I said, we have a big generator. We had it installed in 2005, after Katrina and Wilma left us without power for fifteen days. It cost a LOT of money, and we have to have it maintained regularly, but now, finally, after twelve years of standing by, it is ready, when we really need it, to: break.

Which is what it does after Irma. It breaks big-time. A generator guy examines it and informs us, somberly, the way you would tell a patient he has a terminal disease, that the generator threw a rod. Essentially our generator has transformed itself into a one-ton paperweight. It is no more capable of producing electricity than a Barca-lounger. Apparently all that standing by plumb wore it out.

So now we have no power, no Internet, no phone, no cable, no cell service. One could argue that, in a way, this is a good thing. We have an opportunity to live more simply, like our ancestors, many of whom were dead by age twenty-seven. Without the incessant electronic distractions of modern life, we can, as a family, slow down, reflect, spend quality time together and actually *talk* to each other. And we do! The main topics we discuss are:

- When our electricity will come back.
- How much it sucks to not have electricity.
- The purpose of our existence.

I am of course kidding about that last one. We already know the purpose of our existence: *to be on the Internet.* It's scary, how dependent we have become on technology, how helpless—how *empty*—we feel without it.

As the powerless post-Irma days drag on, we become increasingly anxious, edgy, irritable. We sleep fitfully, we fret constantly, we accomplish almost nothing. And then, late on the fourth day, we are raptured. Our electricity comes back, and within an hour so do our phones, cable and—*Alleluia!*—Internet. Within minutes we are back to leading modern, productive lives, by which I mean checking Twitter every ninety seconds.

So that was how Hurricane Irma affected me and my family. It made us crazy. It utterly disrupted our lives. It caused us to buy lentils.

Now I'll tell you how the hurricane affected Lucy.

It didn't.

Well, maybe it did a little. The first time I took her outside after the storm, with the wind still gusting pretty hard and the landscape littered with tree debris, it took her a few minutes longer than usual to locate an acceptable place to pee.

But that was pretty much it. She didn't go insane before the storm came, because she didn't know it was coming. During the storm, she mainly slept. After the storm she was fine. She had food; she was with the people she loves. That's all she needs to be happy.

Of course this is because Lucy is, not to put too fine a point on it, a dog. She's a simpler creature than I am, and thus her needs are simpler than mine. I couldn't be happy being Lucy; I don't want to live like a dog. I want to enjoy the benefits and comforts afforded by modern civilization: shelter, indoor plumbing, antibiotics, Pringles.

But my needs have gone far past the basics. I am way too dependent on a complex, ever-expanding, fragile network of technological conveniences and diversions. The Internet alone is not enough: I need it to be superfast and available all the time, everywhere. A computer alone is not enough; I need one with a huge amount of "RAM" and "gigabytes," even though I have no idea what those things are. TV alone is not enough: I need a huge screen and a thousand hi-def channels, with everything available on demand. A cell phone alone is not enough: I need one with a screen that has 297 trillion pixels, whatever the hell a "pixel" is. And no matter what I have today, I will need more and better and faster tomorrow, because there will always be cooler gadgets for sale, each one starting out as a technological marvel but quickly becoming, to my mind, a basic necessity.

In short: to be happy, I constantly need more things.

Lucy needs food and family. That's all she needs now; that's all she will ever need.

So here's the lesson she taught me during Irma:

Don't Let Your Happiness Depend on Things;
They Don't Make You Truly Happy,
and You'll Never Have Enough Anyway.

I'm not suggesting that this is an original observation. Wise people have been saying this for thousands of years. I'm also not suggesting you can't get *any* happiness from material possessions. Of course you can. It's nice to have nice things. It's nice to live in a nice house, drive a nice car, wear nice clothes, eat at nice restaurants. It's better to have money than not to have money. It would be silly to deny this.

But there's a limit to the happiness possessions can provide. Somewhere in the vast lifestyle gap between Buddhist monk and Bill Gates, there's a sweet spot, where you have enough stuff to be comfortable, but not so much that it's a burden, consuming most of your attention, leaving little left over for you to pay to your family, your friends, yourself. Where the sweet spot is depends on you, of course, but it's probably a lot closer to the monk than to Bill.

Of all the lessons I've learned from Lucy, this is probably the most obvious. Yet I'm having trouble incorporating it into my life. I have way more stuff than I need, and I keep acquiring more. I own multiple computers. I own seven guitars *and* a ukulele, none of which I can play worth a poop. A few years ago I got into photography so I could take pictures of my daughter's soccer team, which was a fine idea, but somehow I wound up with multiple cameras and a ridiculous number of lenses. In the photography-hobbyist community, I have what is known as "GAS," which stands for "Gear Acquisition Syndrome." What happens is, I'll be looking at some photography website on one of my multiple computers, and I'll see a review of a fifteen-millimeter lens. (Not to get too technical, but: the number of millimeters of a lens refers to how long, in millimeters, something in the lens is, although I have no idea what.) This review immediately gets my attention, because *I don't have a fifteen-millimeter lens.* I DO have both a seventeen-millimeter lens and a twenty-millimeter lens. But I'm thinking I need to buy the fifteen.

At this point you may be wondering, "How often do you use your seventeen-millimeter and twenty-millimeter lenses?"

The answer is, not very often. Hardly ever, in fact. They don't have enough millimeters for soccer.

"In that case," you're wondering, "why would you buy a fifteen-millimeter lens?"

BECAUSE I DON'T HAVE ONE, YOU IDIOT.

Sorry! I don't mean to snap at you. This is what Gear Acquisition Syndrome does to a person's mental processes.

My point is that over the decades I have acquired a great many unnecessary possessions, and I don't know how to go about getting rid of them. No, that's not accurate. The truth is, I don't know that I *want* to get rid of them. I am hostage to them, and to technology in general; I am addicted to these things, as I was reminded during Irma.

I know, intellectually, that I don't have to be this way. I can be happy with much, much less. I know this because when I was younger and poorer, I was pretty happy with way less stuff.

Consider electronics, of which I now own a vast array. I grew up in a household that, like most households in the fifties, had one phone. It was a heavy black metal rotary-dial phone that was wired to the living room wall and shared by six of us. Our phone number was 3119. That's right: four digits, which I still remember, although I cannot tell you where I set my reading glasses down ten minutes ago. It was a very big deal when somebody called long distance. If you answered the phone, and it was the long-distance operator, you'd run through the house, looking for a parent, shouting, "IT'S LONG DIS-TANCE!" in pretty much the same tone of voice you would use to announce that the kitchen was on fire.

Aside from the phone, the high-tech items in the early-fifties Barry household were a radio and a record player. We got our first TV somewhere around 1955. It was a large wooden box with a tiny screen, but it was even more exciting than long distance, because on that screen, we could see, for the first time in our lives, the wonder of: static. We did not get great reception. But we were still excited, because this static was coming *all the way from New York City*. And sometimes, in the swirling gray fuzz on the screen, we could sort of make out an image of . . . Roy Rogers! Or maybe it was Edward R. Murrow. Or possibly it was Roy Rogers's horse, Trigger. There was no way to be sure, but we didn't care. We had television! With *three different channels*, broadcasting three different varieties of static! And we could change channels without getting up, because we had a remote control.

"Phil!" we would yell at our remote control, which was my younger brother Phil. "Change the channel!"

My point is, we didn't have much in the way of electronic diversions, but I managed to have a happy childhood anyway. My friends and I found plenty of ways to occupy our time: we played sports, we rode bikes, we camped out in the woods around Armonk, we told each other jokes, we farted competitively, we blew up a wide array of things with cherry bombs.[23] We had a lot of fun without having a lot of stuff.

I remained relatively possession-free through college. For the decade or so after, I could move all my worldly

---

23   If you owned a decorative lamppost in the greater Armonk, New York, area in the late 1950s or early 1960s, I am truly sorry.

goods in an afternoon, with the help of a couple of friends, some grocery boxes and a U-Haul. I didn't have much money, but I don't recall my finances ever being a cause for unhappiness. I don't recall feeling that I lacked anything really important. I do recall many good times. And what I recall about those times involves people, not things.

But somewhere in my later, more affluent years I fell victim to Possession Creep. I *could* buy stuff, so I *did* buy stuff. And now I'm hostage to it. And as I said, I'm not sure I have the will to do anything about this.

But I intend to try.

For one thing, I'm determined to spend less time on the Internet. I don't need to check Twitter every ninety seconds. Every two minutes is plenty.

But seriously: I waste WAY too much time on the Internet, and a whole bunch of that time consists of my reading something and thinking: *What a moron.* I'm seventy years old; I don't have that much time left. *Why am I wasting it on morons?*

I'm going to read more books. Before I had the Internet, I read books all the time. In recent years, I've become much more likely, when I want to read something, to go to the Internet. I'm going back to books. They're generally less stupid, and they work during hurricanes.

But mainly I'm going to try to cut down on possessions. As a start, I'm going to stop acquiring them randomly. For example, I'm not going to buy the fifteen-millimeter lens that I would probably never use. *Even though it got excellent reviews.*

Also I'm going to try to reduce the mound of stuff I already own, especially all these redundant electronic things. I'm going to figure out which ones I really need, and donate the rest to people or organizations that can use them. I'm determined to clear the clutter out of my life. And I know exactly where I'm going to start.

The lentils.

THE SEVENTH LESSON FROM LUCY

When Lucy was fairly new to our household, we got a Christmas tree, as we do each year in observance of the fact that my wife and daughter are Jewish but really enjoy celebrating Christmas and are thankful to have me as an excuse.

We put the tree up in our living room, where, in accordance with ancient tradition, I spent several festive hours untangling our strings of drugstore tree lights, which had, over the course of the year, formed themselves into a vicious, snarling, basketball-sized wad. After I finally got them strung up, Michelle and Sophie painstakingly festooned the tree with tinsel garlands and red bows and the 2.3 million ornamental tree tchotchkes that Michelle has collected over the years. Then we went out to dinner.

When we returned, Lucy, as usual, greeted us at the door, but she was abnormally agitated—whimpering, frantically leaping up on us, then flattening herself on the floor in the yoga position known as Pancake Dog.

If you're a veteran dog person, you know what Lucy was telling us: she had done a Bad Thing. We hastened to the living room. It looked like a tchotchke bomb had gone off. The tree was down; ornaments were smashed and scattered everywhere. To this day, we don't know who started it. Perhaps the Christmas tree got aggressive, leaving Lucy no choice but to defend herself. All we know is, Lucy felt very, very guilty, and desperately needed to confess to us.

This is typical for dogs: not only do they know when they've done a Bad Thing, but they also admit to their crimes. If you have two dogs, and one of them does a Bad Thing, they will *both* act guilty, because they both feel bad. Also they may have forgotten which one of them did it. They are not astrophysicists. If there were a criminal-justice system consisting entirely of dogs, this is how it would work:

JUDGE DOG: How does the defendant plead?

DEFENDANT DOG: Guilty, Your Honor.

DEFENSE ATTORNEY DOG: I also plead guilty.

JUDGE DOG: Guilty of what?

DEFENSE ATTORNEY DOG: I don't know.

PROSECUTOR AND JURY DOGS: We are also guilty, Your Honor.

JUDGE DOG: Me too!

This ability to feel remorse is one of the many ways in which dogs are better than cats. Cats have the morals of Hannibal Lecter. If you come home and find your cat inside your parakeet's cage, holding your dead parakeet in its jaws, your cat will be like, "Obviously this parakeet committed suicide." Meanwhile your dog, if you have one, will be moping around under the cage going, "I did it! I ate the bird!"

My point is, dogs are honest to a fault. There is no deceit or insincerity in them; they are incapable of lying. If they don't like somebody or something, they will never pretend that they do. You always know where you stand with dogs.

I was tempted to make this the Lesson from Lucy for this chapter. Something simple like: *Never lie.* But I think that would be too simple. For humans, it's more complicated: sometimes lying is the right thing to do. I will give you a real-life example, involving scallops.

One year, during the winter vacation break, my family and my wife's cousin's family chartered a sailboat in the British Virgin Islands. This is a wonderfully relaxing family vacation that I highly recommend to anybody who has children and a sincere desire to squander their college tuition.

It's totally worth it. You wake up each morning aboard a boat anchored next to a lovely palm-fringed Virgin Island ringed by white sandy beaches. You admire the sunrise, have some breakfast, maybe take a dip in the warm, crystal-clear water. Then you weigh anchor, hoist the sails and set off. After an invigorating five or six hours of sailing, you drop anchor next to another Virgin Island. Or possibly you're still next to your original Virgin Island, having traveled a total of twenty-nine linear feet, because sailing is not a speedy form of transportation. There is a lot of zigzagging.[24] In 1492, after two months at sea on his historic voyage to the New World, Christopher Columbus could still, if he squinted, see his wife waving to him from the dock back in Spain. If you want to actually get anywhere via sailboat, you have to employ expert seamanship, by which I mean a motor.

But this doesn't matter in the Virgin Islands, because

---

24 Technically, this is called "keelhauling."

you're not there to get anywhere. You're there to relax and enjoy the natural beauty and consume a rum drink called a "painkiller" that can be used as either a refreshing beverage or an industrial solvent.

The boat we chartered was a catamaran[25] named *Good Vibrations*. Rest assured that we did not operate it. No charter company on Earth would be stupid enough to entrust a valuable vessel to the likes of us. We had a two-person professional crew. The captain was a native of Guyana named Don Fung Fook. That is his actual name, and in addition to being a superb sailor, he is a cool guy with a great sense of humor. This is fortunate, because if you think it's possible to be drinking painkillers on a boat named *Good Vibrations* and not be amused to the point of snot emission at least eight times per hour by the fact that your captain is named Don Fung Fook, then you frankly know nothing about life at sea.

The chef/social director was a native of Germany named Petra Hess who has lived, worked and partied in the sailing world most of her adult life. She is a wonderful person to have with you on a cruise. She seems to know everybody in the Caribbean, and she is an expert

---

25   Technically, a catamaran is "a kind of boat."

social director. On New Year's Eve, she took us and Captain Fung Fook to a party at a restaurant on Virgin Gorda called Chez Bamboo, where Petra, an enthusiastic dancer, had us all gyrating like insane people on a dance floor next to a projection screen—set up near the DJ to provide a sophisticated visual backdrop—that kept flashing the words CHEEZ BAMBOO. Every time I saw this I came close to falling down. It was the most fun New Year's Eve I ever had, and I don't even remember half of it.

Anyway, Petra, in addition to her other talents, is a marvelous, professionally trained chef. It is not easy to create meals in the cramped confines of a sailboat kitchen.[26] In previous sailing trips to the Virgin Islands, we attempted to prepare our own food, and by the second day we were on a diet consisting almost exclusively of Oreos. But Petra somehow created delicious, sophisticated, varied meals for breakfast, lunch and dinner, day after day. At every meal we gorged ourselves, moaning with pleasure and heaping praise on her. She was always asking us what we'd like to eat next, and we were always saying, "You're the culinary genius, Petra! Whatever you make, we're going to love it!"

---

26 Technically called a "scupper."

Which brings us to the scallops.

I am not a fan of scallops. Scallops, along with clams, oysters and mussels, belong to a biological class of organisms known, technically, as Phlegms of the Sea. My feeling is, Mother Nature puts these repulsive slimy things inside shells on the ocean floor specifically to prevent us from eating them. Whereas she puts pigs, for example, in accessible locations such as Iowa, where they can easily be converted into delicious pork products such as "rinds."

Perhaps you think I am being overly squeamish about scallops. Well, perhaps this is because you are unfamiliar with an article from the March 28, 2013, issue of *The Atlantic* by Alexis C. Madrigal titled "Did You Know Scallops Have *Eyes*? Me Neither, but Look."

Yes! Scallops have eyes! In fact they have *many* eyes. According to the *Atlantic* article, a biologist named Sonke Johnsen has studied scallop eyes and has found them to be surprisingly complex. The article quotes this passage about the structure of the scallop eyeball from Sonke's book *The Optics of Life: A Biologist's Guide to Light in Nature*:

> *Why the eye needs two retinas, why it uses a mirror, and why what is essentially a glorified clam needs fifty to one hundred good eyes are open questions that another of my former*

students, Dan Speiser, took on. My favorite experiment of his involved showing scallops movies of food (in the form of particles moving on a computer screen). The scallops, held in little seats, would open their shells to feed if the particles were big enough and not moving too fast . . .

So to summarize what we have learned:

1. Scallops are not merely disgusting wads of mucus: they are disgusting wads of mucus *that can see.*
2. They can sit in seats and *watch movies.*
3. This may explain the popularity of the *Transformers* franchise.

OK, that last point is conjecture on my part. But the first two are scientific facts, and I believe they prove my thesis, which is that we, as humans, have no business putting these things in our mouths. I have long felt this way, but I keep my feelings to myself. I understand that there are individuals who actually like scallops, just as there are individuals who like recreational enemas, or communism, or the song "Copacabana." I feel sorry for these individuals, but I make no effort to correct them.

So I kept my mouth shut when, one evening toward

the end of our week aboard *Good Vibrations*, Petra announced that she was going to make us scallops for dinner. She was excited about this. She said that she had managed to procure some exceptionally good scallops.

Now, to me, the concept of an "exceptionally good scallop" is like the concept of an "exceptionally fun prostate exam." But as I say, I kept my mouth shut. As we sat down for dinner at the table out on the back deck of *Good Vibrations*, I was counting on my family and my wife's cousin's family to shoulder the burden of eating the scallops. Afterward I would join the chorus of voices telling Petra how delicious they were.

Remember the scene in *The Godfather Part II* when Michael Corleone—who is with a group of mobsters in Havana attending a show starring a performer known as "Superman" because of his spectacularly large male endowment[27]—overhears his brother Fredo, who claimed he didn't know Johnny Ola, telling another mobster that he (Fredo) had previously been taken to this same show by Ola, and in that moment Michael realizes that Fredo has secretly been helping Ola's associate Hyman Roth, who wants to destroy the Corleone family and tried to

---

27 Technically called a "yardarm."

have Michael whacked? Remember the look of shock and hurt in Michael's eyes when he realizes that his own flesh and blood has betrayed him?

Well, that is exactly how I felt that night when—after Petra set a large steaming platter of scallops on the table—I began to realize that *my family was not going to eat them*.

OK, that is not entirely true. My wife ate a few. My cousin-in-law Ron Ungerman bravely stepped up and ate maybe six. But the rest of our party, including my own daughter—my own daughter!—totally betrayed me by not eating any. Meanwhile, Petra kept coming out to check on how we were doing. We kept saying, "Great! Yum!"

But there's an old saying in the culinary world: "The platter does not lie." And our platter still had a lot of scallops on it. In fact it seemed to have *more* scallops than it started out with, as if the scallops were reproducing, right there in the melted butter. And if you don't think that cooked scallops can reproduce, may I remind you that you didn't even know that scallops have eyeballs.

We were getting desperate. We were hiding scallops under our salads and side dishes, but there wasn't enough room, because we had eaten almost all of our salads and side dishes. Time was running out. Soon Petra would discover that most of us hadn't touched the entrée she had worked so hard on and was so proud of. We were doomed.

Remember *Rambo: First Blood Part II*, in which John Rambo is parachuted into the jungles of Vietnam, where, without regard for his own safety and generally naked to the waist, he manages, against impossible odds, armed with only a knife and a bow and arrow, plus later a rocket-propelled grenade launcher and an attack helicopter, to rescue a group of American POWs and single-handedly wipe out roughly 80 percent of the Vietnamese armed forces?

Well, that example of selfless courage is very similar to what happened aboard *Good Vibrations* that evening, when my cousin-in-law Ron—who could have simply told Petra, truthfully, that he ate a bunch of scallops, thus throwing the rest of us under the catamaran—heroically piled a large mound of uneaten scallops on his plate and, at great personal risk of being seen, snuck around to the side of the boat and heaved them overboard.

We cannot know for certain what happened next underwater. Perhaps there were live scallops on the seabed beneath us; perhaps, with their numerous eyeballs, they saw our discarded scallops drifting down toward them. Perhaps they were traumatized by this sight. ("My God, is that Gary? THEY KILLED GARY!!")

But this is speculation. What we do know is that just as Ron came skulking back from the side of the boat, empty plate in hand, looking extremely guilty, a figure emerged from inside the boat. Fortunately, it was Captain Fung Fook. He took in the scene with the eyes of an experienced mariner and immediately grasped what was going on. Seconds later, as Ron was hastily sliding back into his seat at the table, Petra emerged. She surveyed the now-scallop-free table, and beamed as we showered her with praise and thanks for the fantastic dinner.

Captain Fung Fook just smiled.

So here is my point: we were not honest with Petra. Essentially we lied to her. But it was one of those lies you tell not to help yourself, but to avoid hurting somebody else's feelings. It's like when your wife asks you if you like her haircut. It doesn't matter if you like her haircut: YOU LIKE HER HAIRCUT.

It's also OK to lie to your wife if she asks you if you were checking out another woman. There are four reasons for this:

1. You don't want to hurt your wife's feelings.
2. You are not seriously interested in the other woman, because you love your wife, but your nervous system forces you to look at the other woman anyway because millions of years of evolution have turned you into a disgusting pig.
3. Your wife knows you're lying anyway.
4. Your wife routinely checks out other men, although you are unaware of this because she uses a secret, utterly undetectable biological ability women have developed—scientists think it involves a combination of estrogen, infrared light and sonar—that enables a woman to accurately assess a man's eye color and package size to the cubic centimeter at night at a range of up to sixty yards *without ever looking in his direction.*

Another legitimate reason to lie is if you're a parent. Say you're watching football on TV, and during a commercial six-year-old Billy asks you what Viagra is. You can't give a truthful answer to this question. For one thing, you have no child named Billy. For another, age six is way too early for a child to be dealing with the concept of erectile dysfunction. The responsible course is to tell the child an innocent lie, such as "I don't know," or "Shut up, I'm watching football," or "Ask your mother."

Likewise if your children ask you if you ever did drugs, you should not answer: "You would not *believe* what you can see if you stare into a candle flame for three hours!" The correct answer, even if *at that very moment* you are rolling a joint, is: "No." (Also correct: "Ask your mother.")

Another scenario where it's OK to lie is when two couples who know each other but are not close friends bump into each other at, say, the movies. After some painfully perfunctory small talk, when it's clear nobody has anything left to say, it's traditional for the women to say, sometimes simultaneously, with sincerely feigned enthusiasm: "Let's definitely get together soon! We always say we're going to, but this time let's really *do* it!" It's OK to tell this flagrant lie because it's way less awkward than the truth, which is: "We have exhausted our supply of mutually interesting conversation topics in under three minutes, so there's no need for us to speak again for a minimum of two years."

Also, if a person asks you if you think he or she is an idiot, it's best to answer no, even if you do, in fact, think the person is an idiot.

Also, if somebody texts you something meant to entertain you, it's OK to text back "LOL" even if you are actually OMA (Only Mildly Amused).

Also, if somebody gives you a gift, you should declare that you're delighted, even if you're not. The only exception is when a husband gives his spouse something that he clearly bought for himself. For example, I had a newspaper colleague whose big Christmas gift to his wife one year was a chain saw. I'm not suggesting here that no woman would want a chain saw; I'm sure there are plenty of women who would cherish receiving a chain saw. But my colleague's spouse was not one of them. She did not pretend to be delighted. My colleague was lucky she didn't use her gift to dismember him.

I could go on, but you see my point: there are some situations when lying is better than not lying. In most of these situations, the primary reason for the lie is not to benefit you, but to avoid hurting the feelings of somebody else. Otherwise, it's almost always better to be honest with people—better for them, and better for you.

So the Lesson from Lucy for this chapter is:

Don't Lie Unless You Have a Really Good Reason,
Which You Probably Don't.

There are two main reasons why you shouldn't lie to benefit yourself:

1. It's wrong.
2. It's stupid.

It's wrong because even if a lie helps you, it deceives somebody else, and it undermines the trust that holds us all together. If we can't trust each other, we can't work with each other, learn from each other, enjoy each other, love each other. Lying makes the world a dodgier, crappier place.

Most of us know this, but a lot of us lie anyway. We figure *our* lies are OK, because we're not *really* bad people, and besides, we're clever, so the people we're lying to won't know. Which may be true in the short run. But if you keep lying, which is an easy habit to get in to, you will become a dodgier, crappier person—untrustworthy, furtive, unsure of who you are, afraid of being exposed. That's bad enough, but it gets worse. If you lie a lot, no matter how clever you think you are, people will figure you out. That's why lying, in addition to being wrong, is stupid: you lose whatever advantage you thought you'd gain from the deception, AND people know you're a liar.

This is especially true if you habitually lie to impress people. Nothing is less impressive than a person who is obviously trying to impress.

People really dislike being lied to. In my experience, they're likely to forgive you for doing something wrong if you admit it; they're far less forgiving if you do something wrong and lie about it. This is one reason why Washington, DC, is wildly unpopular. There is no American institution more monumentally incompetent than the federal government, yet if we are to believe the people in charge of it—I'm talking about both parties—they, personally, have never made a single mistake. Of course my point is that we *don't* believe them; we despise and ridicule them, clever as they believe they are.

So don't be like our political leadership. Be like Lucy. As the saying goes, if you mess up, fess up. Whenever you can, tell the truth. And do not be afraid to say these words:

I was wrong.

I made a mistake.

I'm sorry.

I apologize.

I'm not saying people will always forgive you. But at least they'll know, and you'll know, that you didn't lie to them.

As with the other Lessons from Lucy, I've been pondering whether I need to do a better job of applying this one to my own life. I like to think I'm a pretty honest person. Granted, over the course of my journalism career I wrote thousands of newspaper columns filled with lies, but except for the truly humor-impaired, I think most of my readers knew I was kidding.

In my personal life I try to tell the truth. I think this is one benefit of growing older. Children, even though they're supposed to be more innocent, lie all the time—to impress, to avoid blame or just for the fun of it. As we age, most of us, unless we are destined to join our nation's leadership class, discover the drawbacks to lying, and learn that, if nothing else, it's just *easier* to tell the truth.

So I think I've learned this lesson pretty well, although I can do better. I'm pretty honest, but I'm still, out of arrogance and stubbornness, too slow to admit when I'm wrong, and too reluctant to apologize. I need to work on that. In fact I'll start now, with this apology:

Petra, if you're reading this, I'm sorry for lying to you that night at dinner. It seemed like the right thing to do. I still think maybe it was, at the time, but now I've blown it by revealing what happened in this book. I hope that, since time has passed, and since you know how much my family loves you, you will find this story amusing. But if you don't: I am genuinely sorry. You are a great cruise director and a fantastic chef. We will definitely cruise with you again. And next time, I will try the scallops.

OK, that last sentence is a lie.

EPILOGUE

I'm skeptical about self-help books. Over the decades, on book tours and at book events, I've encountered many self-help authors, and a remarkably high percentage of them did not strike me as competent, good or even necessarily sane human beings.

Years ago, on a local-TV morning show in a midmarket city, I saw a self-help author go in front of the camera and tell the viewers, in a calm, confident, authoritative tone, exactly how they needed to change their lives to become happier, better people. Minutes later, in the greenroom, this author flew into a nasty, screaming, eyes-bulging, water-bottle-throwing rage at his publicist—you would have thought she murdered his entire family *and* ate his cat—because one of his local radio interviews had been canceled.

According to book publicists I've talked to, incidents like this are not uncommon. I'm not saying that all self-help-book authors are hypocritical assholes interested only in helping their own selves. But enough of them are that it's a joke in the publishing world.

So as I say, I'm skeptical about self-help books.

And here I've gone and written one.

In my defense, I intended this to also be a funny book about dogs and people and life in general, and I hope it is. But it's also self-help-y, and—I cannot deny it—maybe even a little preachy in places. So let me stress here that *I do not consider myself a wise person or an authority on anything except maybe the lyrics to Beach Boys car songs from 1963.* I certainly do not consider myself qualified to tell you how to live your life. I decided to write *Lessons from Lucy* because I thought, as a guy getting up in years, that my own life could be happier, and that maybe I could learn something useful about happiness from my aging but consistently joyful dog.

I don't claim that the seven lessons I came up with are amazing, or even original. They are obvious. They are common sense. My problem is not that I didn't know these things; it's that I've done a lousy job of using what I know.

But I'm trying to do better. I'm trying to actually help

myself with this self-help book. So I thought I'd conclude it with a report card on how I've done so far with applying the Seven Lessons from Lucy to my own life.

Lesson One:
Make New Friends.
(And Keep the Ones You Have.)

I've done better with the second part of this lesson than the first. I've been making a point of keeping in better touch with old friends, sometimes calling them purely to say hi, which is something I never, ever used to do. I also hosted a large party for my birthday, which is also something I've never done. Many old friends came, and we partied reasonably hearty for old people; the glow from that weekend stayed with me for months. I love my friends. That's an absurdly obvious statement, but I'm just now, at age seventy, realizing how true it is.

I have not done nearly as well with the first part of this lesson. Unlike Lucy, who remains as outgoing as ever, I still resist meeting new people, let alone becoming friends with them. Apparently I'm not alone. I've been asking guys my age whether they've made any friends in their later years, and they consistently say they haven't. As one of them put it: "I don't *want* any more friends. I'm not sure I want the friends I have." This was a typical response. Maybe it's an older-guy thing.

But I'd like to do better. Maybe I need to take up some activity that would force me to meet people, like golf. The problem there is that the people I'd meet would be into golf. They'd want to talk about their putters, and how they bogeyed an eagle birdie on the fourteenth hole. I already hate them.

See? I have a problem. I need to work on this.

MY GRADE: C

Lesson Two:

Don't Stop Having Fun.

(And If You Have Stopped, Start Having Fun Again.)

I'm doing better with this one. As I write these words the Rock Bottom Remainders, who have not performed for several years, are preparing for a gig at a book festival. I don't mean "preparing" in the sense of "practicing the songs ahead of time" or even "knowing which specific songs we will be attempting to play." I mean "preparing" in the sense of "periodically sending each other emails asking what date the gig is again." But we seem to have it pretty much nailed down, so we will be getting back onstage, a bunch of aging people flailing away at musical instruments, trying to remember the lyrics and getting as funky as we are able given our current medical conditions. So that will be fun.

In my Lucy-inspired quest for fun I also reconnected with the World Famous Lawn Rangers of Arcola, Illinois. My plan was to march with the Rangers in the 2017 Broom Corn Festival; I even talked two of my friends, Mike Peters and Ron Ungerman, both of whom are mentioned in this book, into joining me. Unfortunately that plan was derailed by Hurricane Irma (also mentioned in this book). But I am determined to rejoin the Rangers in 2018. Life is too short to not be part of something that stupid.

I've also been spending more time with my three-year-old grandson, Dylan, who possesses a seemingly infinite capacity for having fun. *Everything* is fun for Dylan. We can spend a highly entertaining half hour just lying on our backs on the floor and slaying each other by taking turns making fart noises. We're kind of like Congress, but more productive.

The point is, I'm definitely having more fun.

MY GRADE: A

Lesson Three:
Pay Attention to the People You Love.
(Not Later. Right Now.)

This is a constant struggle. I try to focus on the people around me, the people I love, but there's always something else I think I need to be doing, and my phone is constantly whispering, "Look at me! *Look at me!*" I still yield to too many distractions, and each time I give away minutes, sometimes hours, that I could be spending with my family, time I'll never get back because apparently it was more important for me to interact with random strangers on Twitter.

But I'm trying, and I think I'm doing better than I used to.

MY GRADE: C+

Lesson Four:
Let Go of Your Anger,
Unless It's About Something Really Important,
Which It Almost Never Is.

This one is also a constant struggle, but I'm working hard on it. For example, when some idiot cuts me off in traffic, I no longer allow myself to become consumed by rage, which is both unproductive and unhealthy. Instead, using a technique perfected by Zen masters, I take a deep breath, then calmly, even serenely, blast the idiot into a cloud of glowing particles with the fantasy Zen phaser cannon mounted on the front of my car. Then I exhale, and I'm fine.

Also I almost never argue about politics anymore, and I have pretty much stopped watching the nonstop freak-out-a-thon that is cable-TV news. I am a far happier person for it. The world may be going to hell, but then again it always was.

MY GRADE: B–

Lesson Five:
*Try Not to Judge People by Their Looks,
and Don't Obsess Over Your Own.*

I'm doing OK on this one. The older I get, the less judgmental I am about how other people look, because every morning I observe my own personal appearance in the mirror and I think, quote, *Yikes*. I've reached the point where I think I'm looking pretty sharp if all my nose hairs are approximately the same length.

MY GRADE: B–

Lesson Six:
*Don't Let Your Happiness Depend on Things;
They Don't Make You Truly Happy,
and You'll Never Have Enough Anyway.*

I'm doing pretty well here. In the past year I haven't purchased a single new camera lens to accompany all the other camera lenses I own that I almost never use. Also I am holding steady at seven guitars. The only new electronic device in my life was given to me by my son: it's Alexa, a computerized virtual woman who inhabits an Internet-connected box. Alexa sits on the counter, patiently waiting for me to give her commands or ask her things. Like I'll say, "Alexa, what's the temperature?" And Alexa will answer: "Right now it's eighty-three degrees in Miami." I already know this, of course; it's *always* eighty-three degrees in Miami. I'm only asking to keep Alexa from getting bored.

I think Alexa is a nice addition to our household, but Michelle is not a fan. She and Alexa often do not see eye to eye. Like if I tell Michelle we need beer, she'll say something like, "We already have plenty of beer," whereas if I tell Alexa we need beer, she'll immediately respond, "I've put beer on your shopping list." So there's some tension between the two. I frankly think Michelle's a little jealous. I tell her that Alexa could never replace her, and I mean it, despite the fact that I can tell Alexa I want to hear virtually any song—for example, "The Game of Love" by Wayne Fontana and the Mindbenders—and she will instantly play it, which is a capability that Michelle does not possess. I'm just saying.

MY GRADE: B+

Lesson Seven:
Don't Lie Unless You Have a Really Good Reason, Which You Probably Don't.

I think I'm doing OK here, too. I still tell lies, of course, but they're usually little white lies told for a good reason, like when I tell somebody who doesn't look great that he or she looks great, or when I tell the Internal Revenue Service that I have fourteen dependents.

Just kidding, IRS! Please do not audit me! As I have accurately stated on my tax returns, I have only eleven dependents, including Alexa.

But seriously, I'm doing OK on this lesson.

MY GRADE: B

So according to this report card, I'm averaging somewhere around a low B in my ongoing effort to apply Lucy's lessons to my life. Lucy, of course, has an A-plus. She's still a happy and loving dog, all day, every day; she's a joy to be around. It's hard to imagine life without her.

But I have to, of course. Lucy's almost eleven; she doesn't have many years left. When she goes, she'll go gracefully, the way dogs do—without complaint, self-pity or regret. Which is another lesson I can learn from her, though I'm not ready for it yet.

Meanwhile I'll cherish the time I have with Lucy, and do what I can to make her last years as pleasant as possible. Toward that end, Sophie and I have been lobbying Michelle to get a puppy, so Lucy will have somebody to play with and be with when we're not around. Michelle has been resisting us, her argument being that puppies can be a lot of hassle. It hasn't helped that some friends of ours, who recently got two Lab puppies, have been giving us progress reports that always contain the phrase "there's urine everywhere."

But Sophie and I—especially Sophie—have not given up, and I think eventually we'll prevail. We'll get a puppy;

for now, I will refer to him as Buster. And at first Buster will, in fact, be a hassle. We'll have to housebreak him, and teach him not to chew stuff or climb on the furniture. But soon enough, with us nagging him and Lucy serving as a role model (except as regards the white sofa), he'll learn what's right and what's wrong.

And then he'll start teaching me.

ONE LAST LESSON

This chapter wasn't supposed to be here.

Lessons from Lucy was supposed to end with the epilogue you just read. That was the conclusion of the manuscript I sent to my editor, Priscilla Painton. The book was done: I'd covered the lessons and tied them up with a nice neat bow. *Lessons from Lucy* was edited and proofread; advance publicity copies were sent out to the media; a book tour was planned.

Meanwhile my daughter, Sophie, was getting ready to start her freshman year at Duke. She was excited: Duke had been her first choice, and she was thrilled when she got accepted. Michelle and I knew we'd miss her, but we were happy for her, and looking forward to our new life as empty nesters. We were going to kick it off with a trip to Las Vegas.

We had plans. Life was orderly. Life was good.

On Saturday, August 18, two days before we were going to take Sophie to Duke, she woke up paralyzed from the waist down.

Just like that. Overnight. She could not move her legs. She couldn't even wiggle her toes.

She was paralyzed.

Sophie hadn't been sick that she was aware of. We'd gone out to dinner the night before to celebrate with her grandmother. Sophie later told us that during dinner her legs felt a little tingly. But she figured it was just nerves, anticipation, excitement.

Our first thought, that Saturday morning, was that she was having some kind of anxiety attack. *It has to be that*, we thought. *She's a healthy young woman. There's nothing wrong with her.*

We told her that. We told ourselves that.

People don't just become paralyzed overnight.

It's just stress.

She's fine.

But we soon realized that, whatever it was, it wasn't going away. Michelle called Sophie's doctor, who told us to take Sophie to the hospital. I lifted Sophie onto a wheeled desk chair, rolled her through the house to the garage, then lifted her into the car. We drove to Baptist Hospital, about fifteen minutes from our house. We got a wheelchair and rolled her into the emergency room waiting area.

Sophie was not panicking. If I'd been in her situation—if I suddenly couldn't move my legs—I'd have been freaking out. But Sophie was calm, even joking a little. I told her she'd be walking out of there before the end of the day. I believed it.

She's fine.

After a few minutes in the waiting area, we were met by a neurologist who'd been called in by Sophie's doctor. The neurologist examined Sophie, asked her some questions. I was waiting for the neurologist to tell us not to worry, it was just nerves.

But she didn't. She said Sophie needed an MRI scan. Right away.

We went to the MRI area. The techs lifted Sophie onto a special gurney, asked if she had any metal on her. She took off her earrings and gave them to Michelle. The neurologist was urgently typing something on a computer and talking to the techs. Twice she used a word that, until then, I had never heard a real doctor say—only actors playing doctors.

The word was "stat."

As they were about to take Sophie into the MRI room, we kissed her on the forehead and told her we'd be right outside. She gave us a nervous little smile and said OK. Then they wheeled her away.

We went into the waiting room and sat. There was a TV on, but we ignored it. We didn't talk much; we didn't know anything. We just sat there, waiting. I felt as though I was barely breathing.

After a while the neurologist came into the waiting room. Her face was somber. She said the MRI techs weren't finished yet, but she'd seen enough that she felt she should talk to us. I will never, ever forget the words she said next.

"This is not good."

Sophie apparently had an autoimmune disorder called Transverse Myelitis.[28] Something—maybe a virus, maybe something else—had triggered her immune system,

---

28 I'm not a doctor, so please understand that everything I say in this chapter about medical matters represents my very limited, English-major understanding of what happened.

which attacked the invader, but then went on to attack Sophie's spinal cord.

The neurologist said they were going to begin treatment immediately.

She said they would do everything they could so Sophie would—these were her words—"have a chance to walk again."

I remember leaning forward in my seat as the neurologist spoke, putting my face in my hands, closing my eyes, trying to absorb what I was hearing.

A chance to walk again.

The neurologist went back to the MRI room. Michelle and I looked at each other, both of us thinking the same thing: *This isn't happening. It can't be happening. She's going to college in two days.*

Michelle was on her phone, googling Transverse Myelitis. Here's what she found:

One-third of the people who get TM have "good or full" recovery.

One-third have "fair" recovery, but are left with "deficits."

One-third do not recover. They live their lives in wheelchairs.

This can't be happening.

The neurologist came back and told us she was taking Sophie out of the MRI so she could begin treatment. We hurried out to see Sophie. She was frightened now, trying to grasp what was happening to her as the neurologist explained the situation. Michelle and I tried to be reassuring, but nothing we could say could refute the obvious truth.

This is not good.

The hospital people put Sophie on a transport gurney and wheeled her off through the maze of corridors. Michelle and I walked behind, fighting back tears, our stomachs hollow pits, following our girl—our girl who was supposed to be going to Duke—as they took her to the Critical Care Unit.

Within minutes Sophie was in a hospital bed, catheterized, connected by wires to monitors, an IV drip connected to her arm through which they were giving her heavy doses of steroids to reduce the inflammation in her spinal cord. They installed a port in her groin for a procedure called plasmapheresis—sort of like kidney dialysis—in which the antibodies are filtered out of the blood plasma. They did other things as well. The strategy, as I understood it, was to suppress Sophie's immune system enough so that her body could start healing from the damage it had done to her. Because she was young and fit—she'd played soccer since she was four—she was getting what they call aggressive treatment. Every few minutes, it seemed, a doctor or nurse would come in to check the monitors, draw some more of Sophie's blood, ask her more questions, give her another pill, another shot.

Meanwhile Michelle and I were trying, in our shell-shocked state, to figure out what we needed to do—who we needed to call, what we needed to cancel, what we needed from home. We didn't know how long Sophie would be in the hospital. We didn't really know anything.

This can't be happening.

Our life became a sleepless nightmare. Michelle stayed next to Sophie—she would not leave her side—while I was in and out of the room, talking to people, making arrangements. I wandered the halls of the Critical Care Unit, intercepting visitors[29] and making phone call after

---

29 These were mostly friends who showed up at the hospital unannounced, wanting to see Sophie. Their intentions were good, and I love them all, but: It's a bad idea to drop in unexpectedly on people undergoing intensive medical treatment. They're already dealing with physical and emotional trauma; they don't need the added burden of social interaction. So here's an etiquette tip: If you want to visit a hospital patient, check first to make sure that person is up for visitors, and if he or she isn't, don't take it personally. Remember: It's not about you.

phone call. I remember calling the guy at the storage place in Durham where we'd shipped Sophie's college stuff, telling him that my daughter was in the hospital, that we wouldn't be picking up her things on Move-In Day, that she wasn't going to be starting Duke with the rest of the Class of 2022. I broke down. I was embarrassed, sobbing into the phone to a complete stranger.

"I'm sorry," I said.

"It's all right," he said. "I hope your daughter's OK."

"Thank you," I said, hanging up, because I was breaking down again.

I broke down a lot. Not when I was in Sophie's room; then I did my best to be Mr. Positive, Mr. Jokey Dad. But in the hospital halls, calling people, having to explain the situation over and over, I kept losing it.

I called my son, my brothers, our friends, told them what had happened, heard the shock in their voices.

All of them asked the same thing: "Is there anything I can do?"

But there wasn't anything they could do. If there was anything that could be done, Michelle and I would have done it. But there was nothing. It's an especially cruel kind of torture, to watch, helpless, as your child suffers.

You would do anything to make it better. Every parent knows this: You would gladly, in an instant, trade places with your child.

Take me. Paralyze me.

But you don't get that choice. You have to watch your child enduring pain, trying to cope with a terrifying situation, and you can do nothing for her except try to be upbeat, even though you have been given no real reason to be.

A chance to walk again.

The doctors kept asking Sophie the same questions.

"Can you wiggle your toes?"

"Do you feel this?"

Again and again, Sophie had to answer no, she couldn't wiggle her toes. No, she didn't feel anything.

Over and over and over, she had to say this. Over and over and over, day after day, while we all stared at Sophie's bare, motionless toes.

One-third do not recover.

Sophie never complained—about the questions, or the treatments, or anything else. She was scared, but she never panicked. She never showed bitterness, never lashed out. She never once asked, "Why me?" She smiled at everybody who came in. She thanked every doctor and nurse, even the ones who had just given her a shot. She was stronger and braver than I could ever be.

So was Michelle. She never left Sophie's side, a mother guarding her young. She slept as best she could on a recliner chair, night after night, so she could be there at 1:48 a.m. and 3:37 a.m. and all the other seemingly random times when hospital people came into the room to do still more medical things to Sophie.

I went home at night, to check the house, get the mail, walk Lucy (we had somebody look after her during the day) and try to sleep. But—this is another thing every parent knows—you don't really sleep when your child is suffering. It's almost worse if you do fall asleep, because when you wake up, there are a few seconds when everything seems normal. Then you remember, and that is an awful feeling. Your stomach goes hollow again, and you wish, at least for a moment, that you could go back to being unconscious.

When you're in that situation, you see two worlds. There's Normal World, the one everyone else seems to be in—the one you used to be in—where people are going to work, buying groceries, watching the TV news, helping their kids with homework, getting their cars fixed, laughing, gossiping, making plans and doing all the other things people do in normal life. In Normal World, it's possible to be happy.

When your child is suffering, you're in a different world entirely, Hospital World, a constricting, bleak, isolated place. Normal World concerns don't matter to you at all. You don't care about the news, what the president said, what his critics said, what the news people thought about it. You don't care if your car needs servicing or your roof has a leak. You don't make plans. You don't want to see anybody. You don't care what you're wearing, or if you've slept, or when you last ate.

All you care about is your child. All we thought about, all the time, was Sophie, Sophie's legs, Sophie's toes. When Sophie was sleeping, Michelle would whisper to me, "I just want her to get better. I don't want anything else. I would live the rest of my life in a tent. I just want her to get better."

I tried hard to hope, but I was never far from despair. On Sophie's third day in Critical Care, the Monday morning that we were supposed to have flown with her up to Duke, I was driving to the hospital via a route that took me past Sunset Elementary School, which Sophie attended from kindergarten through fifth grade. That

Monday happened to be the first day of public school in Miami-Dade County. I stopped at a red light in front of the school and watched as some parents walked their children across the street. Michelle and I walked Sophie across that same street, at that same spot, a thousand times. Sitting at the light, seeing those little kids, with their hyperactive little-kid legs, walking where my happy, healthy little girl once walked, I was overwhelmed by a feeling of hopelessness, of dread. At that moment, I wanted to just disappear from the earth.

Which is another choice you don't get, as a parent. You take a deep breath, and when the light turns green, you continue driving through Normal World to Hospital World, to be with your child, because that's all you can do.

Hospital World is a strange, unsettling place. You mark the passage of time not by hours and minutes, or even day and night, but by procedures—the next shot, the next blood draw, the next round of plasmapheresis, the next X-ray, the dreaded spinal tap—which can happen seemingly at any time, nobody is ever sure exactly when. You wait. It is mainly what you do.

You have no privacy. People keep coming to your room: nurses, food-service people, housekeeping people, hospital administrators, occupational therapists, physical therapists and, of course, doctors—in our case, many of them—neurologists, nephrologists, hematologists, infectious-disease specialists, internists and more. Hospital people observe a protocol when they visit: They knock twice, then usually before you can respond, they enter, from early morning until late at night and beyond. Sometimes you know them; sometimes you don't. After a while you get used to the unending parade of medical visitors, unquestioningly submitting to whatever they're there to do.

My running hospital joke—in my role as Mr. Jokey Dad, trying to cheer Sophie up—was that I was going to start walking around the hospital, knocking twice on patients' doors and announcing that I was the staff herpetologist. I'd go in, ask the questions that doctors ask—"Any changes? Experiencing any pain?"—maybe check the patient's pulse, then leave. I seriously believe that 95 percent of hospital patients would totally accept me as legit, especially if I wore khakis and a collared shirt. If I could figure out how to get the insurance companies to accept herpetologist bills, I'd clean up.

I spent a lot of time trying to entertain Sophie, because in between medical intrusions, Hospital World is boring. You can watch TV, but it's daytime TV, which means you have to choose between cable-TV-news people endlessly chewing the same cud, or astoundingly mindless reality shows such as *Say Yes to the Dress*, in which brides-to-be agonize endlessly over which wedding dress to buy, a decision they appear to take far more seriously than, say, who their husband will be.

We watched many episodes of *Say Yes to the Dress*, as well as a show called *Extreme Couponing*, which deals with people who are obsessed with using coupons to save as much money as possible on their grocery bills, even though this strategy means coming home from the supermarket with twenty-seven cases of Tabasco sauce and a sixty-three-year supply of tampons.

We binge-watched *Friends*, *New Girl* and a trivia game show called *The Chase*. Sophie and I also got into crossword puzzles, and I will state in all modesty that we became quite good at them. I don't know if many eighteen-year-olds know that when the clue is "Singer Fitzgerald," the answer is "Ella," but Sophie Barry definitely does.

That was how we passed the time in Hospital World, being as mindless as possible until it was time for the next procedure, the next shot, the next doctor knocking twice and asking Sophie if she could wiggle her toes.

Which she still could not. A week went by, and it felt as though Sophie had been asked to wiggle her toes a hundred times. Each time we would all stare at her bare feet.

Nothing.

"I'm sorry," Sophie would say.

"It's OK!" we'd say. "It'll come."

But with each day, our doubts grew. At least mine did. I didn't say so to Michelle, but late at night, as I lay in bed, the awful thought kept forcing its way into my sleep-deprived brain.

What if this is it?

During this time Michelle and I were getting hundreds of texts, emails and phone calls from family and friends, wanting to know how Sophie was doing. "We're thinking about her all·the time," they said. "We're praying for her."

These were not perfunctory prayers: Sophie is truly beloved. I know that, as her dad, I can't be trusted to give an objective opinion on this, but anybody who knows Sophie would tell you the same thing: She is a genuinely good person. She's also smart and funny, even edgy, but what really distinguishes her—and has since she was a little girl—is her character. She has never been cruel or mean-spirited to anyone. She is generous, thoughtful, gracious. She would never let down a friend, and she has many, many friends. She's just *good*.

So when word got around about her condition, the shock was greater than if it had been, say, me. People could not accept the *wrongness* of this thing happening to this extraordinary young woman, this beautiful soul. And so they prayed for her, and sent messages expressing love and hope and good thoughts, and an aching, anguished need to be able to do something more.

This is from an email that my friend Ridley Pearson sent me in the first days:

> *All my prayers, man. I know you don't think they help, but I'm just at a loss and have to do something.*

Ridley was referring to the fact that I'm an atheist. Here's how I answered his email:

> *Hey, I'll take all the prayers you got. I'VE been praying. I keep saying "Please." I don't know if anybody's listening, but I'm saying it.*

That was true. I was saying "please" all the time—in the hospital hallways, in the car, alone at home. *Please let*

Sophie be OK. To be clear: I was still an atheist. My feeling was that if there really was a benevolent all-powerful being capable of healing Sophie, that being would never have let this happen to her in the first place. But I was saying "please" anyway. Just in case. Just—in Ridley's words—to do something.

I did other things, too. Weird things, good-luck bad-luck things, like always entering and leaving the hospital via a certain route, or avoiding looking at certain photos on the hospital walls. Really. I knew this was irrational, even crazy, but I did it anyway. Just in case.

Ten days passed. Sophie's legs still showed no movement. I wanted to put a sign on her bed, to keep the doctors from asking: NO, SHE CAN'T WIGGLE HER TOES. WE'LL LET YOU KNOW.

We tried to keep her distracted, inside our little Hospital World cocoon. We had our inside jokes, about the incomprehensibility of the hospital schedule, about *Say Yes to the Dress*, about friends who kept sending us food in quantities far larger than we—or for that matter the Pittsburgh Steelers—could possibly eat (we have a lot of Jewish friends). Sophie also welcomed distractions from the therapy dogs that volunteers brought to the hospital to cheer up patients. Here's a picture of Sophie getting some therapy from a dog named Clue, who visited on Sophie's tenth day in the hospital.

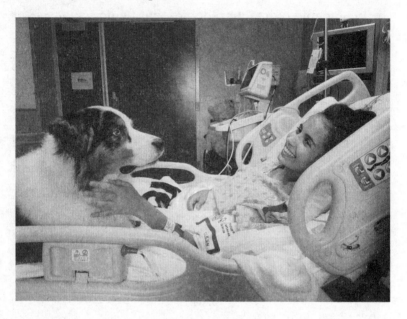

The morning after this picture was taken, I was driving to the hospital after another night of little sleep. I was stopped at a light in South Miami, waiting to turn onto U.S. 1, when my phone rang. It was Michelle.

She said, "Sophie moved her leg."

I don't know what Michelle said next, because I was shouting YES! YES! YES! over and over, and then I was crying so hard I had to pull off the road. This may sound melodramatic, but it's true: That call from Michelle was the happiest moment of my life. I didn't really know, until then, how terrified I'd been that I would never hear those words.

I wiped my eyes, composed myself and drove to the hospital way too fast (although I still was careful to enter the building via the good-luck way). I ran to Sophie's room and stood with Michelle, looking at Sophie's legs, as Sophie concentrated until her left knee clearly moved a half inch sideways, then back, then sideways and back again.

Sophie said, "I'm doing that."

Then I was crying again, but I didn't mind that Sophie saw me, because it was happy crying.

It was only one leg, and it was only half an inch. She still couldn't walk; she couldn't even sit up. There were still no guarantees that she would recover. But something—the medicine, the prayers, Clue the therapy dog—was making Sophie better. Now we had reason to hope.

And from that morning, our hope got stronger each day, as Sophie continued to improve, one tiny muscle movement at a time. We celebrated each new sign of progress; we rejoiced when, at last, she could wiggle her toes for the doctor.

In another sign of progress, Sophie was disconnected from the IV drip and monitor wires that had kept her tethered to the hospital bed. She was also granted grounds privileges, which meant we could take her, in a wheelchair, out of the hospital building and roll her around the property. On our first outing, September 1, we left the hospital by the same doorway that Sophie had entered back on August 18, which was only two weeks earlier but seemed like forever ago. Escorting Sophie in her wheelchair was a posse consisting of her brother Rob, sister-in-law Laura, nephew Dylan, Michelle and me. Sophie led us in a grounds-privileges chant:

> SOPHIE: When I say "grounds," you say "privileges."
> Grounds!
> POSSE: Privileges!
> SOPHIE: Grounds!
> POSSE: Privileges!

And that's how we rolled, Sophie and her badass posse. Here's a group selfie Sophie took during that outing:

Yes, we look like idiots. But now we were hopeful idiots.

After three weeks, Sophie was moved to the neurological rehabilitation unit, where the focus shifted from pumping medicine into her body to teaching her muscles how to work again. Four or five times a day, she worked with physical therapists and occupational therapists, painstakingly relearning physical actions that most of us perform without thinking, like sitting up, or reaching for something without falling over.

Michelle and I went to the rehab gym to watch her and cheer her on, the way we watched and cheered for her in a thousand soccer games. Except that instead of cheering her for a good pass, or a defensive play, we were cheering for each sign of progress in her recovery—like when, strapped to a rehab contraption, she stood. She wasn't standing unassisted—without the contraption, she'd have fallen—but she was on her feet again, and the sight made our hearts soar.

Her next contraption was a kind of sling with wheels, which enabled her to walk, sort of. From there she moved to a series of walkers, which got smaller and smaller as Sophie was able to rely more and more on her legs.

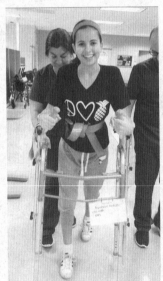

Until finally came the wonderful day when Sophie, without any help, walked. She was a little wobbly, and she couldn't walk far.

But she could walk again.

After five weeks in the rehab unit, the doctors declared she was ready to go home and become an outpatient. And so, forty days after entering the hospital, Sophie left the same way she entered—in a wheelchair—but once outside she stood and walked to the car.

I'm writing this a couple of months later, just before Christmas 2018. Sophie still has some healing to do and is still doing physical therapy. She has more doctors, and more procedures, ahead of her. But she's strong, and walking really well, even driving, and living a nearly normal life again. In January she'll begin her new stage of life as a freshman at Duke. There has never been a student more eager to get started.

That's Lucy in the background.

The last four months have been, by far, the most difficult of my life. Physically, I lost a bunch of weight and went through a rousing case of shingles, which is a funny name for a disease that otherwise has very little amusement value. Emotionally, it has been brutal. Things are a lot better now, but I am never, ever going to forget the anguish, and the fear, of those dark early days.

I don't mean to be self-pitying here. It was much, *much* tougher for Michelle. At least I went home to sleep, spending a few hours outside of Hospital World. Michelle never left. She never quit, never flagged, no matter how tired she was after all those nights on that hospital recliner. She was Mom Strong. She is the second-strongest person I have ever known.

The strongest is Sophie. Through this whole ordeal, no matter how scary or uncertain her situation was, no matter what medical discomfort or indignity she was subjected to, she never complained. Think about that: *She never complained.* She never let herself get too far down; she never lost her sense of humor. Michelle told me that late one night, when they were almost asleep, Sophie said, "You know, Mom, this would make a really good college essay."

A number of people have said to me that, in a way, this experience will ultimately help Sophie, because it will give her perspective, make her resilient, teach her to deal with adversity. I know these people mean well, but my feeling is, Sophie was already a remarkably kind and wise person. She didn't need to be taught a lesson, especially not in such a cruel manner.

I also didn't get much comfort from the people who

told me that God does things for a reason, and what happened to Sophie was part of His master plan. Again, these people meant well. But when you're watching your child suffer—your thoughtful, kind, generous child who never did anything to hurt anyone—it doesn't help to be told that her suffering has some greater purpose not knowable to you. At least it didn't help me.

This is not to say I learned nothing from this experience. I definitely learned a lesson—the most important lesson I've ever learned. It's a lesson that came to me gradually, and one that I was reluctant to accept at first. But I have come to believe it, and I pass it on to you now:

Be grateful for what you have.
(It's probably more than you think.)

When Sophie first got sick, gratitude was the last emotion I could have imagined feeling. I was shocked, afraid, angry; I saw nothing to be thankful for.

That changed early on, even before that miracle morning when Sophie moved her left leg. It started with the intense and sustained outpouring of love that flowed toward us from family and friends all over the country. I could feel that love, and it gave me strength at a time when I desperately needed to be strong. So I am very grateful to those people for their love and support. And, yes, for their prayers.

I'm also grateful for Sophie's doctors, skilled and dedicated people who, unlike me, could actually do something to help her. In our shock and fear and confusion, we needed to trust them, and they justified our trust.

I'm grateful for the Baptist Hospital staff, especially the nurses. If you've ever been hospitalized, you know that the doctors pop in and out, but the nurses stay. They're the ones who watch over you; they're the ones you call when you need help. Their job is physically and emotionally demanding, and at times unpleasant. But they never let us down. Every nurse Sophie had, and there were many, was encouraging, *caring*. I don't think you can do that job and not be a good person.

Same for the physical and occupational therapists: They were wonderful to Sophie, always patient, but always challenging her to do more, and always cheering her progress. The day Sophie left the hospital, we hugged them the way you hug family, because they felt like family. I will always be grateful for their dedication.

I am deeply grateful to Duke University. I used to hate

Duke, because the Duke men's basketball team was always beating basketball teams I rooted for. I stopped hating Duke when they accepted Sophie, but I still didn't *love* Duke. Then came the morning when I had to call the dean of students, Sue Wasiolek, from the Critical Care Unit, and tell her, my voice choking, that Sophie would not be arriving with the rest of the Class of 2022. My fear, when I made that call, was that Sophie, who had already, overnight, lost so much, would somehow also lose Duke, the thing she had been most looking forward to. I will never forget what Dean Sue (as everyone calls her) said: "Tell Sophie not to worry. Duke has been here a long time. We'll be here when she's ready." So I was able to give Sophie one bit of positive news when there wasn't anything else good happening. And now I love Duke.

Of course what I am most grateful for is seeing Sophie walk again. It's such an ordinary act, walking; I never gave it any thought until Sophie couldn't do it. Then it became the most precious thing in the world. Now I'm grateful every time I see Sophie enter a room. I suppose I'll get used to it, but I don't think I'll ever take it for granted again.

I know that what we've been through with Sophie, as

hard as it has been, is not the worst thing that could have happened. Michelle and I talk about this a lot: There are parents who never see their children walk again. There are parents whose children die. There are many people, of all ages, dealing with horrific, incurable medical conditions. I don't mean to compare our situation to theirs.

But I do feel qualified, based on our experience, to offer this lecture:

If you and your children are basically healthy—if, when you wake up in the morning, you can get out of bed—you should be grateful for that. If you have family and friends who love you, you should be grateful for that. Don't take these things for granted: They are the most important things in your life.

I'm not saying you should ignore your problems, or the problems of the wider world; I'm saying *keep them in perspective*. Don't let your happiness depend on the news, or the stock market, or office politics, or traffic. Don't let people who don't know you tell you how you should feel. Don't believe that the world is terrible, or wallow in outrage or victimhood, just because some politician or radio-talk-show host or college professor tells you to. Decide for yourself how your life is going, and when you make that calculation, start with the fundamentals: Are you walking around? Do you have people you love? Do they love you? Do you have enough to eat? A place to live?

If you have those things, you have a lot to be grateful for. If you also have laughter in your life, and music, maybe a nice sunset once in a while, you're blessed. Try to remember that the next time you're feeling stressed or unhappy. Things could be a lot worse.

Anyway, that's my last lesson. I didn't learn it directly from Lucy, though the more I think about it, the more I realize that I could have. Lucy, like most dogs, overflows with gratitude. She knows what's most important in her life—the people she loves—and she never takes us for granted, which is why each time we return to our house, no matter how brief our absence has been, she greets us with quivering, unbounded joy. During those bleak nights when I drove home alone from the hospital, the happiness Lucy radiated when I opened the door always lifted my sagging spirits. She was a true comfort to me, following me from room to room in our too-empty house, keeping me company, keeping close to one of her people.

That's all dogs want, really: to be with us. It's why

they're here, and why we love them. Somehow, over thousands of years, our two species developed this special, wonderful relationship, which once was based on utility, but now, for most people, is about love. It's a beautiful thing. One more thing to be grateful for.

ABOUT THE AUTHOR

Dave Barry is the author of many bestsellers, including *Dave Barry's Complete Guide to Guys, Dave Barry Turns 40* and *Dave Barry Is NOT Making This Up*. A wildly popular syndicated columnist, Barry won the 1988 Pulitzer Prize for commentary. He lives in Miami.